TRANSFORMATIONAL
PUBLIC SERVICE

TRANSFORMATIONAL PUBLIC SERVICE

PORTRAITS OF THEORY IN PRACTICE

CHERYL SIMRELL KING
LISA A. ZANETTI

M.E.Sharpe
Armonk, New York
London, England

The story in the Comment "Setting the Stage" is from Jack Zipes, *Creative Storytelling: Building Community, Changing Lives* (New York: Routledge, 1995). Copyright © 1995 by Routledge. Used by permission of Routledge/Taylor & Francis Books, Inc.

The poem "To be of use," in the Comment "To Be of Use," is from *Circles on the Water: Selected Poems of Marge Piercy* (New York: Knopf, 1982). Copyright © 1973, 1982 by Marge Piercy and Middlemarsh, Inc. Used by permission of Alfred A. Knopf, Inc., a division of Random House, Inc.

Library of Congress Cataloging-in-Publication Data

King, Cheryl Simrell.
  Transformational public service : portraits of theory in practice / by Cheryl Simrell King and Lisa A. Zanetti.
    p. cm.
  Includes bibliographical references and index.
  ISBN 0-7656-0947-9 (cloth : alk. paper) — ISBN 0-7656-0948-7 (pbk. : alk. paper)
  1. Social action—United States. 2. Public administration—Moral and ethical aspects.
  3. Social action—United States—Case studies. 4. Public administration—United States—
  Case studies. 5. Political participation—United States. I. Zanetti, Lisa A., 1960– II. Title.

HN65.K483 2005
361.2'0973—dc22   2004017170

Printed in the United States of America

The paper used in this publication meets the minimum requirements of American National Standard for Information Sciences Permanence of Paper for Printed Library Materials, ANSI Z 39.48-1984.

∞

| BM (c) | 10 | 9 | 8 | 7 | 6 | 5 | 4 | 3 | 2 | 1 |
| BM (p) | 10 | 9 | 8 | 7 | 6 | 5 | 4 | 3 | 2 | 1 |

Contents

Part IV. Transforming People

Acknowledgments

This book would not have been possible if not for, first and foremost, the public service practitioners profiled and others we talked with along the way. They gave us their time and energy; we are in their debt. The deep and abiding friendship and respect between the coauthors was also crucial to our work. This book took a long time to come to fruition—the patience and faith of our editor at M.E. Sharpe, Harry Briggs, was central to giving this work the space and time it needed to evolve. Still, even with a wonderfully supportive editor and excellent profilees, we would not have pulled this off without the care and respect that comes with a relationship that weathers the test of time and the challenges of living in our complicated world. One of the guiding principles that emerges from this work is that strong and respectful relationships are containers for personal growth, are essential to our healthy functioning, and are central to the possibility of practicing transformative work. We can personally attest to this.

We are also deeply appreciative of all of those who helped us along the way: the students in the MPA program at The Evergreen State College and students at the Harry S Truman School of Public Affairs at the University of Missouri, Columbia, who reviewed chapters and listened to the ideas, providing important feedback that helped shape our work. In particular, we wish to thank the 2004 first-year Core students at Evergreen who read and responded to a draft of the manuscript. Our friends and colleagues helped us in ways too complex to enumerate. We wish to thank in particular Guy Adams, Joan Bantz, David Boje, Richard Box, Adrian Carr, Bob Cunningham, Judith Dahn, Alexis Downs, David John Farmer, Larry Geri, Terry Gibson, Louis Howe, Gail Johnson, Sandra Kensen, Russ Lehman, John Nason, Alan Parker, Tricia Patterson, Nita Rinehart, Grace Ann Rosile, Linda Moon Stumpff, Pieter Tops, Pete Williams, Sarah Williams, Matthew Witt, Robert Zinke, our colleagues at the Tilburg School of Politics and Public Administration, Tilburg University, the Netherlands (where Cheryl had a sabbatical during the time this book was being conceptualized and written), and our international colleagues affiliated with the Danish government-funded DemoNet. The University of Missouri-Columbia provided summer research support for Lisa as did The Evergreen State College for Cheryl. Many thanks to audiences at conferences who listened to these ideas come together and contributed to the evolution of this book. We are deeply appreciative of Daniel Kana Shephard, who carefully edited the final draft of this manuscript and helped shape a critical revision. Every work needs a good editor—we all thank you, Daniel.

Cheryl is especially appreciative of Helena Meyer-Knapp, her "parallel writing partner," who sat across the dining room table during much of this writing. Helena embodies compassionate wisdom and inspires the same, we hope, in our work. Lisa is especially grateful to Charles Hayman, whose "bohemian" nicely checks her "bourgeois," and whose unconditional support and confidence pulled her out of many dark nights. She is also thankful for her family and especially her parents, Allen and Janet Zanetti, who continue to be sources of wisdom and inspiration.

We both acknowledge our families and our loved ones, especially our children. Carl Jung said that children are our opportunities to meet ourselves. Assuming we have the privilege to imagine these as opportunities and as places for us to grow and thrive, there is no better way to come face-to-face with oneself than through loving and nurturing children. We deeply appreciate the presence of Kate, Becca, and Stephanie in our lives; we are sure that much of who we are can be attributed to them. And, like most children of working parents, they often have to sacrifice their needs to our work; they have done so with graciousness and strength we could only hope to mirror.

Prologue

Wide Awake and Dreaming

I say to you today, my friends, that in spite of the difficulties
and frustrations of the moment, I still have a dream.
It is a dream deeply rooted in the American dream.

—Martin Luther King Jr., "I Have a Dream."
Delivered on the steps of the Lincoln Memorial
in Washington, DC, August 28, 1963.

Richard Linklater's film *Waking Life* (2001, Fox Searchlight Pictures/The Independent Film Channel Productions) beautifully addresses the liminal states of wakefulness and dreaming. There are two scenes in the film that speak to our work. In the first scene, four young men are walking down a street, talking. They are making strong statements about power, oppression, and consumerism: "Society is a fraud." "Where there is fire, we will carry gasoline." "Live as if something depends on one's actions." "Immerse ourselves in the oblivion of action." The young men see an old man, on a pole, and ask: "Hey old man, what you doing up there?" He answers, "Eh, I'm not sure." "Need any help getting down, sir?" the young men ask. "Umm, I don't think so." The young men walk away. "Crazy bastard," one of them mutters. Another says, "No worse than us. He's all action and no theory; we're all theory and no action."

The scene changes: the main character of the film meets the dreamer. "Are you a dreamer?" the dreamer asks. "Yeah," says the listener. "I don't see too many around lately," says the dreamer. "Things have been tough lately for dreamers. They say dreaming is dead. . . . No one does it anymore. It's not dead, it's just been forgotten. Removed from our language. Nobody teaches it so nobody knows it exists. The dreamer is banished to obscurity. I'm trying to change all that and I hope you are too by dreaming everyday, dreaming with our hands and with our minds. Our planet is facing the greatest problems it has ever faced. Ever. So, whatever you do, don't be bored. This is absolutely the most exciting time we could possibly hope to be alive and things are just starting."

We wrote this book because we believe in the importance of theory-based action and action-based theory. Because we believe in the importance of being wide awake and dreaming; of dreaming every day with our hands and with our minds.

Dreaming while sleeping is the stuff of the American experience: journeys taken in search of streets paved in gold and of fountains of youth. Being wide awake and dreaming is another state altogether. It means being fully present in the world and conscious of the pain and contradictions of living yet, nonetheless, dreaming with our hands and minds to make a better world. This better world is not measured by the size of our homes, bank accounts, or the cars we drive but, instead, by equality, justice, empowerment, democracy, and community.

The idea for this project came out of a collaboration that produced the book, *Government Is Us: Public Administration in an Anti-Government Era* (King, Stivers, & Collaborators, 1998). In *Government Is Us,* the collaborators attempt to show that American government is *not* us and deconstruct some of the reasons why this is so. At the heart of the work in that book are the deep disconnects resulting from governments being far removed from the people governed. The collaborators argue that these disconnects can be changed through citizen and government engagement and coproduction.

Our work here builds on Lisa's contribution in *Government Is Us,* where she defined transformative public administration as:

> [a] practice of public administration that reconnects the knowledge of expertise with the knowledge of experience. It does so by combining technical proficiency with a normative foundation that values the wisdom gained from common sense and personalized observation. Transformative public administration allows the public service professional to function as a critical specialist who recognizes that neutrality and objectivity have a dark and troublesome side. It is a practice of interested science that is conducted with the purpose of furthering a more inclusive, substantively democratic polity. (Zanetti, 1998, p. 112)

A transformative administrator recognizes that power relations that are socially and historically constituted fundamentally influence ideas and thoughts. That is, the dominant characteristics of western culture, which privilege certain races, classes, and genders, are human constructions that have been built over centuries of uncritical acceptance. These can, however, be challenged and changed by those willing to take on the task.

A transformative administrator also understands that facts cannot be isolated from values or normative assessments of the world. Because we cannot simply observe the world, but instead continually interact with and influence it, our values and experiences color our observations. When we are aware of these influences, we can act to correct certain tendencies—such as the tendency to accept the superiority of expert knowledge in all instances.

An administrator working from a transformative perspective recognizes the potential for all citizens to be <u>democratic philosophers</u>. Each individual has the choice to draw on his/her experiences either to substantiate the status quo, or to recognize the contradictions and work to create new ways of thinking about the world and putting those new modes of thought into being.

Finally, a transformative administrator appreciates how mainstream (instrumental) thought has the effect of reproducing and reinforcing the status quo (Kincheloe & McLaren, 1994). A critically enlightened and sympathetic administrator can play a crucial role by providing the administrative access necessary to bring about change based on experience as well as expertise. S/he can act as an interpreter and facilitator, but s/he can also act as a transformative agent by assisting others to articulate concerns, voice needs, and implement community-developed strategies for change.

In the years since the publication of *Government Is Us,* we have met many people across the world whose lives center on redressing the wrongs perpetuated by deep disconnects among and between citizens and their governments. As we listened to their stories, we heard them say that public service (in both governmental and nongovernmental organizations) *can be* and *is* transformational (transforms institutions, practices, and people's lives and experiences) in ways that serve democracy, engagement, and social and economic justice. The public service they practice is collaborative, humanistic, emancipatory, inclusive, and diverse.

Their work represents best practices or exemplars of transformational public service being done on the margins of public administration. Much attention is given in the literature to mainstream best practices and/or exemplars. We believe it is time to give attention to forms of best practice that exist somewhat outside the mainstream of public administration.

What we have found in our work (and in our own lives) is that people who practice transformational public service often are alone in a crowd, confronting and standing against the dominant crowd as it surges one way or another. This aloneness in the face of surging counterdirectional force can be difficult, draining, and disheartening. We hope that in the (re)telling of the stories of some who are practicing transformational public service, we will feel less alone in our work.

There are others like us out there. And we are making a difference. We want transformative practitioners to be seen, acknowledged, and named. Naming bestows recognition. Recognition, in turn, often generates legitimacy. These practices are not invisible and they are legitimate.

In the traditions of social movements, stories are at the heart of political change. As Couto (1993, p. 61), indicates, narratives "mobilize a group to attempt political change [and] provide deep and lasting insights into the need and methods of change to individuals who lead social movements or support them despite risks to themselves." Lisa Disch notes that storytelling is an important genre that creates spaces for transformation; it is through the telling of the stories that we hope to create more transformation. "A well-crafted story shares with the most elegant theories the ability to bring a version of the world to light that so transforms the way people see that is seems to never have been otherwise. . . . Storytelling invites critical engagement between a reader and a text and, more important, among the various readers of a work in a way that the impersonal, authoritative social science 'voice from nowhere' cannot" (Disch, 1993, p. 665).

In this book, we seek to tell some stories. We will tell stories about theory and stories about practice, with the hope that this storytelling will generate the possibilities for transformation. We start with our own stories.

Cheryl's Story

As I write, I am in a public library in Toledo, Ohio. I was called home on a family medical emergency and found this neighborhood library in my quest for solitude and respite from the difficult family work. I did the same during my childhood: found refuge and respite in the neighborhood library. Where would kids like me be without the services libraries offer to everyone, regardless of race, class, creed, privilege, or abilities? Where would we be without *public* service?

Frozen in the land of lack.

I've spent the last few early mornings walking my mother's neighborhood. The houses are small and modest. People are, generally, "house-proud." Their houses and yards are well maintained and cared for. Fences are for the numerous dogs, not people. People lean over fences to talk to their neighbors. There are no sidewalks, but that doesn't discourage people from walking or kids from riding their bikes. Kids walk or bike to school in the morning and back again at the end of the day.

My mother and stepfather have lived in their house for just a short time. They know all their neighbors in every direction. The neighbor behind and the neighbor next door helped them move their garden shed and get it situated in the backyard. The man who built their deck is the brother of another neighbor. The side neighbor's 19-year-old son hangs off my stepfather's car door, chatting with him. The 10-year-old child who lives behind them helps my parents cut their grass and sits on their porch afterward, watching time pass. My mother helps a neighbor secure housecleaning jobs. They share their food and the fruits of their gardens.

This is community, in the old "barn raising, bring in the crops" sense of community (Kemmis, 1990). The people in the community pay attention to one another. They lean on one another. They watch out for each other. They talk to each other. They work together. They need each other.

At the same time, they are deeply suspicious of those who do not look like them (white working class). Still, they are working against lifetimes of racism to be open to the people of color who have recently moved into the neighborhood. Every house (no exaggeration) has a faded "United We Stand" poster in a front window. The house of the Middle Eastern neighbors has three such posters, one in each of the three front windows. And a "For Sale" sign in the front yard. The Middle Eastern neighbors have learned their lesson well—work even harder to convince others that you are not different and get out as fast as you can when things get too hot. This is, essentially, the story of my familial life.

While this is not the neighborhood in which I grew up, it is remarkably similar. And the people who live there are remarkably similar to the folks in my neighborhood of origin. My parents, like many others, worked hard to keep food on the table and a roof over our heads—there was neither time nor energy for political talk or action. Additionally, there was no room for discourse or dissension. My father ruled with an iron fist and we learned to not make waves. My father's orientation came not out of ignorance but, rather, out of fatigue. Making waves made a hard life that much more difficult. Life was already almost too difficult to bear—better to do what you need to do and/or what you are told to do.

Our life was not the romanticized life of an activist working class upon whose backs labor and other social movements were built. Although we come from solid "hillbilly" roots, we were not "radical hillbillies" like those tutored by Myles Horton at the Highlander Center. We were educated from a very early age to accept our powerlessness. We learned to be unconscious. Doing otherwise was wrongheaded and dangerous.

What I've learned on this visit back to my hometown is that the lives of my family members are very much determined by the "lacks" that often define working class life: lack of resources, lack of efficacy, lack of a sense of empowerment, lack of education and access to information, lack of critical thinking. At this stage in the game, in mid-life, these lacks have a very strong hold on most of my siblings. The lack of opportunity to move against the flow of lacks has created lives and situations that are hard to change. To come to consciousness is risky and potentially dangerous.

Yet, to see the lives of my family members and their neighbors only in terms of lack is to rob the people and their communities of their souls and deny all they are not lacking—community, place, connections with others, and a deep sense of rootedness. While those of us living our lives on the other side of the tracks may not lack for resources or power or efficacy, we lack many of the things that make up community in my mother's neighborhood. Our fences are for people; we don't know our neighbors very well; we don't need one another; we often feel isolated and unmoored in our deeply individualistic lives. Lubrano (2003) states that one of the significant differences between the working and middle classes is individualism; in general, individualism is discouraged in the working class while it is at center in middle and upper class life.

What is it that we can learn from each other, from the other side of the metaphorical tracks? What do we find when we spend time in the in-between of these two worlds—a place I inhabit, to both my delight and dismay? This is a place Lubrano (2003) calls "limbo," where people with working class roots straddle the two classes, never feeling at home in either place. This limbo is a place of problems for Lubrano's interviewees, yet also a place of significant opportunity.

Learning comes through consciousness: through waking up *and* dreaming. Through being awake and recognizing the ways that race, class, gender, privilege, and other categories of "otherness" intersect with the stuff of life. Being awake through an awareness of the emotional, psychological, and physical work one must do to be in this world in ways that are not bound by the shadows of our life experiences. Dreaming through steadfast faith that working toward greater democracy and social and economic justice will lead to a better world. And, because I am privileged to walk between two worlds (my family of origin and the world I have created for myself), I know that this work must be done together with those who live the injustices daily.

As a result, I find myself most aligned with those who practice participatory inquiry, a form of research/social organization that comes out of the critical theory school. (Read on for more on theoretical perspectives.) I am also deeply pragmatic in that I believe process is *the* point: it is through the working together that we work things out. I'm also deeply pleased to find that I am coming, full circle, to my original training in psychology in the ways that depth psychology (a Jungian approach) influences my approach toward action. One of the contemporary streams in depth psychology is in the area of transpersonal, public, or community psychology. Here, psychological scholars and practitioners are just beginning to address the question of how our individual psyches and psychological states affect and are affected by the political and social worlds. It is a stream of psychology that goes beyond the individual to situate the self in the greater political, social, and economic context. It moves the work "on the couch" beyond the individual realm (Samuels, 2001a). Andrew Samuels calls on us to renegotiate what we mean by politics so we can engage the issues of empowerment and disempowerment in a more psychological way. It is not enough to do our own work on the couch, so to speak; we must do our work within the context of the world. It is not enough to practice individually: no person is an island; eventually, we all are called upon to practice within the world.

I call myself a "critical pragmatist." As such, I practice "educational facilitation" (Fischer, 2000). In the classroom and the field my role is not to promote a political agenda or to shape followers of a particular dogma, but to work with others to develop the skills and perspectives needed to practice their own brands of critical pragmatism. I seek to work with people so they can transform themselves and work toward transformation. The desire is not to force a particular ideology on others, but to work, together, to build the conditions within which others have the power to make their own decisions about their lives. Frank Fischer (2000, p. 191) says it best:

> For participatory researchers firmly committed to democratic values, educational facilitation and political proselytizing are geared to fundamentally different objectives. Political ideologists, accepting their beliefs as the one true way of thinking about the world, proselytize with a predetermined definition of the successful outcome; they simply dismiss diverging views as wrong thinking, bad faith, or false consciousness. By contrast, the facilitator may passionately advance ideas about how people should learn and act but must present such ideas to learners for the same kind of critical scrutiny to which the educator has subjected other views of which he or she is personally critical. The end of the encounter, in other words, is not the acceptance by the participants of the facilitator's preordained values and beliefs. Rather, it is to pose problems and questions for critical dialogue and group consensus formation.

The Jungian theorist James Hollis (2001) tells us that we are called to live our lives "*here,* in *this place,* in *this time,* in *this arena*" (p. 68; emphasis in original). For Hollis, we are meant to live life, here, in a certain way, defined by forces that are transcendent to consciousness.

> Such a life will seldom arise from the design of one's ego . . . [and] means living the life one is summoned to, not the life envisioned by the ego, by one's parents, or by societal expectations. . . . Whatever one's fate may have in store, the task, if we are up to it, is to . . . become as nearly like ourselves as we can manage. *Amor fati* is, after all, even amid defeat and confusion, a form of love. To love one's fate is to embrace the loathsome

frog, kiss the suppurating wound, accept the ignominy of defeat, and yet find that somehow one has been blessed. (pp. 68–69)

This blessed life is not easy, as the stories of the people profiled in this book attest. The "American dream" of my youth (and the modern consumption-based rendition) required that one dream while asleep (or unconscious). The dreaming of transformational public servants requires being wide awake, "dreaming everyday, dreaming with our hands and with our mind," and to love one's fate while doing so. "This is absolutely the most exciting time we could possibly hope to be alive"—this here, this time, this arena—"and things are just starting."

Lisa's Story

In many ways, my early life experience was the inverse of Cheryl's. I come from a long line of public servants: my father was a career officer in the U.S. Navy; my mother devoted her professional life to public school education and counseling; her father was a mail carrier; her mother was a public school teacher. Two of my three siblings have chosen some form of public service, as have I. I also come from a family that values higher education: there are three Drs. Zanetti—a cousin, and my mother, who earned her Ed.D. at the age of 60 (and made us very proud), and myself. All my siblings, and my father, have earned advanced degrees.

But my family was also defined by the immigrant experience. My paternal grandfather was born in the town of Cortina, in northern Italy, and immigrated alone to the United States around the age of 11. He married a woman who was born in the United States, but whose parents and siblings had emigrated in the late 1890s. She and my grandfather built a life, and scratched together a living, working as a housemaid and cleaning woman (my grandmother), ran a grocery and butcher shop, and later, a farm in New Jersey. Neither had any formal education beyond the sixth grade, although my grandmother loved to read. (One of my most precious possessions is a set of her beloved Horatio Alger stories.) My father attended college only because he was able to earn a soccer scholarship. The military was his ticket from the working class into the middle (and later, the upper middle) class. The Navy sent him to Harvard for his MBA, and later to the Industrial College for the Armed Forces (ICAF). He was part of the generation that computerized the Naval Supply Corps, and retired as captain after twenty-five years.

My childhood was typical of a "military brat" in that we moved every two to three years. Unlike Cheryl, I have primarily virtual roots—it is probably not a coincidence that I was born in the year Marshall McLuhan coined the term "global village" (McLuhan, 1960). At the age of 3, I was flying for two days in a propeller plane to our posting in Hawaii (didn't everyone do this?). I attended a public high school and a state university, the College of William and Mary in Virginia—part of the so-called public ivy league. For the most part, I did not have to work my way through college, except to earn extra spending money. After college, I attended Georgetown University's School of Foreign Service. I loved Washington and thrived on being in the corridors of power, even in a small way. I anticipated a life and career in the Foreign Service, or at least in the upper levels of the State Department or the Office of the U.S. Trade Representative.

But life often has other plans for us, and in my case, I took a very traditional woman's path by following my then-husband's job transfer to Oak Ridge, Tennessee. I was "radicalized" during my Ph.D. education when I took a year-long course in qualitative research methodology that was cotaught by John Gaventa, of the Department of Sociology, and Fran Ansley, from the School of Law, at the University of Tennessee. Both John and Fran subscribed to the education philosophy of Paulo Freire (1970/2000), and both had been active with the Highlander Research and Education Center, originally founded as the Highlander Folk School in Tennessee (www.hrec.org) by Myles Horton and Don West. (West left within a year and later founded the Appalachian South Folklife Center in West Virginia— www.folk lifecenter.org.)

Part of this course involved working with local community groups. Because I had only virtual roots, I had never had a strong sense of community— at least, not in the physical sense. I have written about my experience in my chapter from *Government Is Us* (1998). Because it was so foundational, I reproduce a segment here.

> When I worked with [a community group] and attended community meetings, I felt ostentatious as an outsider in appearance, dress, speech, background, and life history—a distinction that at times made me deeply uncomfortable. The irony was palpable: Perfectly comfortable walking the corridors of power in Washington, I was brought to adolescent speechlessness . . . at the prospect of interacting with seemingly ordinary community members. It was a humbling experience. . . . How could my veneer of academic knowledge and my professional experience in government contribute to their efforts? . . . Schooled in a culture of meritocracy and accreditation, I could not figure out how to earn for myself the credentials possessed by these organic intellectuals.
>
> Although I did not recognize it until later, such painful experience produced a certain epiphany. Perhaps that same insecurity is the source of many an expert's retreat to the comfortable crutch of objective knowledge,

although most might be highly unwilling to admit it. Having worked so
diligently to acquire our academic and professional accolades, we don't
enjoy being challenged by the quiet and powerful voice of experience. . . .
Yet . . . if we admit to our discomfort in surrendering the status of expertise, we might be surprised to see what we learn. (Zanetti, 1998, p. 118)

This experience was, for me, pivotal. It re-formed my understanding of
ontology, epistemology, and philosophy, and, by extension, formed my research agenda and approach to pedagogy. I had begun my doctoral studies
with the intention of specializing in administrative law, gravitating, however,
toward the fields of political theory and public administration. Drawing on
my experiences as a public servant, I wanted to explore the options for administrative action—specifically, asking whether there was a place for public servants to act with a sense of critical consciousness. Closely intertwined
with the question of administrative latitude is the issue of organization and
community change. What role can the public administrator play in creating
different forms of interaction at both the micro and macro levels?

My own affinity has been for an ontology and epistemology informed
by critical theory. When I discovered critical theory, it seemed I had been
partly living it all my life: always the outsider even while living, and participating, in a particular community. It was easy for me to see contradictions, although I never expected to do much about them. (Why should I?
I'd be leaving soon, anyway.)

As I embraced critical theory, however, I became uncomfortably aware of
the contradictions in my own life. If I wanted to *practice* critical theory, I
could not continue to live in my materially comfortable, upper middle-class
life. Working to resolve these contradictions has taken the better part of a
decade, and is still in progress. I struggle every day with my bourgeois roots—
having to admit, to my dismay, that I more often fit David Brooks's (2001)
description of a "bobo": a bourgeois bohemian. But, I have made conscious
choices to try to walk away from the dominant discourse/consciousness in
all its ramifications.

For a long time, this journey took me to a place that, to many, appeared
apathetic. I had always followed politics and worked as a sometime volun-
teer in various campaigns. I took my young daughters with me to into the
voting booth to emphasize the importance of political participation. In Tennessee, however, I encountered the phenomenon of belonging to a permanent political minority. I became frustrated, then thoroughly disillusioned,
with a political system that considered it "fair" for my views to have no
direct representation (majority rule, winner take all). It occurred to me that
my vote effectively sanctioned an electoral system that I had come to view as

illegitimate. I stopped voting—an action that, when I revealed it at a Public Administration Theory Network conference, caused gasps of indignation and outrage. After all, isn't voting our number one civic duty? I finally voted again in the national election of 2000—only to be even more discouraged, not only at the outcome but at the "failure" of the Green Party to qualify for public campaign financing.

I am still an agnostic when it comes to the efficacy and legitimacy of our electoral process. This is a prominent reason that I share, with Cheryl, the desire to move the conversation that began as a result of *Government Is Us* to another level. We believe that good theory happens at the "nexus of the real and the ideal . . . at the in-between of theory and practice" (King, 1998, p. 167).

One of the most intriguing characteristics/opportunities of critical theory, I believe, is its potential to connect broad, general social concerns with the "micropolitics" of the manner in which social discourses are articulated. In a recent article I used the term micrologies to illustrate this phenomenon (Zanetti, 2002). I find it particularly resonant to encourage individuals to develop their capacities to act as "organic intellectuals" as they recognize and articulate social contradictions, imagine alternatives, and then put these alternatives into practice (a philosophy I also use in my teaching, through dialogue and through the use of techniques from Augusto Boal's Theatre of the Oppressed).

I have also embraced Jungian psychology to explain certain dynamics at the interpersonal level. In particular, I find this framework illuminating in exploring the various dimensions of gender. I agree that, archetypally, the father's house represents the dominant content of a culture's collective consciousness, as well as dominance in the form of tyranny and fear. There is little question that contemporary organizations remain edifices constructed in the image of the father's house. The article articulates barriers to conscious femininity in organizational contexts, drawing on psychoanalytic theory and personal experience to explore some of the social and psychological structures that contribute to the repression of feminine attributes.

What is needed in our world today is practical knowledge, "counterhegemonic consciousness," and political action brought about by establishing a "democratic tension" between the formal knowledge of the academic researcher and the popular knowledge, personal experiences, feelings, and spiritual practices of communities. What will be specifically articulated in this text, which was not specifically articulated in *Government Is Us,* is the focus on praxis—on action and reflection to transform our experiences as administrators, public servants, and citizens. We acknowledge and accommodate the understanding that human activity is both determined by external structures and capable of transforming them. In effect, then, this is as much a text on social change as it is a text on public administration.

Intentions of This Book

We seek to accomplish three interrelated intentions in this book: (1) to show that the time is ripe for practicing a kind of public service that seeks to transform people and institutions in a way that focuses on social and economic justice; (2) to embed this transformation in theory (portraits of theory); and (3) to illustrate the already existing practices of critical theory (portraits of practice) such that public service practitioners can see themselves in the stories of others and imagine/be inspired to continue their work, even when it feels as if they are working against all odds. Our thesis is convoluted but may be summed up simply by the following: Transformational public service is an essential balm for the ills of our contemporary state of being; it is already being practiced and, as such, there are models for those of us seeking to be transformative in our work; and, the capacity to practice transformational public service comes from doing one's own work, individually and within our institutions of governance (both governmental and nongovernmental).

As the title indicates, in this work we have attempted to show the already existing interrelationships between theory and practice. There is a strong temptation to erase theory from books intended for practitioners and students of public administration. The false dichotomy of theory and practice is constantly reified in the practice and study of public administration. Yet, theory is always behind practice—or, as a colleague says, practice is always in front of theory. They are inextricably intertwined. To pretend otherwise is to continue to give credence to the theory/practice dichotomy. As our profilees say, theory cannot be divorced from practice, particularly practices that have the potential to transform institutions and the lived experiences of those touched by institutions serving the public interest.

A note about jargon: in writing this book, we struggled with how much we should strip the theory of its theoretical language. We want readers to read our book with little to no struggle—our intention is to make theory accessible. Therefore, we seek to make our writing accessible to the reader. At the same time, however, to strip the theory of all philosophical language is to, in a way, rob both the reader and the theory of some of the essence of this material and would create a very different text from that which we have made here. Therefore, we have attempted to find what the Buddhists call a "middle way": to be accessible and to do so in language that easily translates across all theory. To aid the reader, we have included a Glossary. When the reader initially encounters a word that is in the Glossary, the word will be underlined.

We have profiled five public service practitioners who work inside government: Evelyn Brom and Sheila Hargesheimer, Human Services Department, Domestic and Sexual Violence Prevention, City of Seattle (see endnote, p. 44); Gary De La Rosa, project coordinator, Human Relations Commission, City of Los Angeles; Douglas MacDonald, secretary, Washington State Department of Transportation; and Claire Mostel, Citizens' Academy coordinator, Dade County, Florida. We have also profiled three public service practitioners working outside of government, as consultants or in nongovernment organizations: Greg Coleridge, executive director, Northeast Ohio American Friends Service Committee; Joseph Gray, president, JEG Associated Consulting; and Randy Scott, principal, ACCESS, Inc.

All of the practitioners profiled work at different levels—some are at the frontline (street level); some are in formal leadership positions within their agencies or organizations. Some do administrative/policy/advocacy work; some do legislative work. Regardless of their setting or level, all are practicing transformative public service.

One additional note: we are aware that this book is United States–centric. While we have both been indelibly influenced by our international work, we consciously chose to focus on public service in the United States. We do not intend to perpetuate the myth that as it goes in the United States, so goes the world. As the traditions upon which our work rests tell us, we need to do our work at home before we begin to try to do it elsewhere. Therefore, we have focused on home.

Comment

Setting the Stage

Many years ago, there lived a king and queen who did not allow their subjects to learn to read and write. "The dumber they are," they said to themselves, "the easier they are to rule." So they posted signs all over their kingdom: "Beware of the Big, Bad Storyteller!"

You see, in those days, storytellers gave people ideas free of charge, and the king and queen knew that ideas lead people to think, and thinking people might have ideas of their own, and soon they might want to learn to read and write, or even put their ideas into action to govern themselves. So the king and queen were quick to spread nasty rumors about storytellers and claim that they twisted people's minds and shrunk their heads.

So fearful did the people become that it was easy for the king and queen to convince their subjects to give them their money for protection and to build a huge fortress out of straw, wood, and brick so that they would be protected from the ferocious storytellers. The fortress was so large that is could house all the people in the kingdom. So whenever a storyteller was seen on the horizon, the king would ring a bell from the tall tower as an alarm and all his subjects would run from the streets and fields as fast as they could to save themselves from the big bad storyteller.

Since storytellers rarely go to places where they are not invited, they stopped visiting this kingdom. That is, until one day when a mighty good and curious storyteller became lost and found his way into this realm. When the king saw him coming with his telescope, he sounded the alarm, and the people were scared for their lives. They made a mad dash for the gigantic house, and when they we all inside, the king and queen locked the door tight, right in the face of the storyteller. When the storyteller knocked, the king asked, "Who's there?"

"It's just me," said the storyteller, "Let me in."

"Not by the hair of your chinny chin chin!" cried the queen, and she commanded all her subjects to repeat: "Not by the hair of your chinny chin chin!"

"Well then," said the storyteller, "I'll huff and I'll puff, and I'll blow your house in. Then I'll tell a tale. To smash this jail. And when I'm through, good-bye to you."

So the storyteller huffed and puffed a glorious tale that filled the people with wonderful ideas and excited their imaginations. When he was done, the house came tumbling down with a crash and a thud. So frightened were the king and queen that they fled the land, never to be seen again. On the other hand, the people were surprised to see that they were unhurt, and they realized that the storyteller was not as mean as he was supposed to be. To their delight, he began telling them even more stories, which the people liked so much that they have passed them on to their children and their children's children up to this very day.

And this, my friend, is why we are just as wise as we are today.

(Zipes, 1995, pp. xxi–xxii)

Storytelling is an ancient art that works, according to Jack Zipes (1995), at many levels. At the first level is the story itself—the content of the story and the "moral" buried within. Stories can also be empowering. From stories, we learn to tell our own stories and, in turn, make ourselves and our lives (Witherell & Noddings, 1991). And, stories and storytellers can intervene and subvert, often in subtle ways. As Zipes (1995, p. 10) states:

The storyteller intervenes, and in the best of scenarios, the storyteller subverts. The children cannot carry on their normal routine exactly as they have done before, nor can the teacher. They must adjust in some way, must reflect consciously or unconsciously, especially if the storyteller has been sensitive to their needs and has actually animated them to ponder who they are and where they are.

Like the little child in Hans Christian Andersen's "The Emperor's New Clothes," storytellers are truth tellers and wise souls. As the story goes, this child is the only one who steps up to the naked king and tells him the truth. The child is wise beyond his years. The child's words, "exposes the ridiculous nature of power and the shame of the community. They clear the picture, enabling everyone to understand what is happening" (Zipes, 1995, p. 224).

In his work, Zipes invokes the critical theorist Walter Benjamin's notion of storytelling as a sharing of wisdom and a method of exposure for the benefit of the community. Zipes says:

The genuine storyteller must feel the urge to divulge what it means to live in an age when lies often pass for truth in the mass media and the public realm. The storyteller must feel the urge to contrast social reality with a symbolic narrative that exposes contradictions. From this contrast, the storyteller gives birth to light, lightens our lives, and sheds light on the different ways in which we can become our own storytellers. (1995, p. 225)

We believe the stories that follow of real people practicing transformational public service shed light on the ways we can, ourselves, become our own storytellers and practice transformational public service. The people portrayed are storytellers themselves—each of them in their work and in their lives seeks to contrast social reality in ways that expose contradictions. They work with people (citizens, community members) to imagine different ways of making our realities.

There are quite a number of public servants practicing transformational public service; probably more than we would initially imagine. Resources and other constraints limited us to undertaking seven profiles with eight public servants.

Three of the practitioners profiled work outside of government agencies, in nonprofits or as independent contractors involved in community-based or legislative work. Five work within government agencies, at the state, city, and county levels. We did not, intentionally, leave out people working at the federal level. Yet, most of the people we have met over the past few years who practice transformational public service do so at local, regional, and state levels or as independents, in nonprofits or community-based organizations. This kind of work is deeply local. This is not to say that transformational work is not happening, or cannot happen, at the federal level (one only needs to think of civil rights, affirmative action, environmental law and protection, and myriad federal laws and administrative practices that have transformed our daily existence). It may well be, however, that transformational work at the federal level is fundamentally different from the kind of transformational work done at the community level.

The people profiled were interviewed during the summer of 2002, either by phone or in person. Our participants worked closely with us throughout the process, reviewing the interview transcripts, reviewing the chapters, and submitting their own writing in response to several key questions. Their writing is interspersed throughout the chapters. In addition, we have woven our thoughts around the stories in sections we call "comments." Some comments are short; some are lengthier, depending on the topic.

In painting their portraits through their stories, we try to capture the spirit of our participants, as well as, in the tradition of storytelling, the spirit of their stories.

Part I

Citizenship and Governance

Transforming Citizenship

Greg Coleridge
Executive Director
NE Ohio American Friends Service Committee
Akron, Ohio

Greg Coleridge seems to be everywhere in Akron, Ohio. Wherever there is an important issue of social or economic justice on the front burner, there is Greg. For Greg, public service is

> that essential element of existence that involves working beyond ourselves, given we are social creatures. It's acting beyond our own immediate environment, our own immediate family, and our own immediate social circles, on behalf of the common good. Public service is helping the world around us, which by doing so helps ourselves by making us more human. We have an obligation to work on behalf of the community at large. We have a responsibility to be publicly engaged to improve our community in tangible ways to the extent that we can. How we do that, of course, is a function of our particular genetic makeup along with the skills and abilities we acquire along the way. There is no magic single way. There are thousands, if not millions, of potential ways this can be accomplished. However it is done, the premise is that we have the social responsibility and duty to work for improvement, good, justice, sustainability, peace, and nonviolence beyond our own immediate sphere.

Akron, Ohio, is Greg's hometown. Like many Akron hometown boys, he is a child of immigrants. His parents were born in what became Yugoslavia: his mother in Montenegro, his father in Serbia. His parents' families embodied an immigrant ethic: hardworking people working together (in a community) to achieve middle-class existence. At the center of this is the belief that an honest living comes from honest effort; only the wealth that you yourself generated is legitimate and honorable. If you are going to make it, you have to outwork the people around you.

Greg was significantly influenced by the activism of his parents. His father was active in the rubber workers union. Greg grew up hearing about the

> ## In Their Words
> ### Greg Coleridge
>
> *What would you like to tell others about what it is like
> to do the work you do?*
>
> Working for the American Friends Service Committee (a Quaker-related social action organization), the work I do for peace, justice, and sustainability is both thrilling and frustrating. I have the opportunity to work along with and on behalf of many selfless, courageous, resourceful, creative, and compassionate human beings. This is inspiring as well as thrilling. It's also thrilling to help create and implement educational and action programs which plant seeds of social change that every so often bear fruit in achieving some type of tangible "victory" or "win." Frustrating is the realization that I lack personally, and at the moment with other social change activists, the time, energy, and resources to sufficiently counter the mammoth power of the media, other business corporations, and the government, which shape public policies, manipulate perceptions, distract attentions, co-opt former allies, adapt themselves in superficial ways in response to criticism, and/or simply ignore popular pressure.
>
> It is also a constant struggle to find the right place between responding or reacting to immediate social problems that arise and maintaining one's long-term plan for social transformation.

formation of the union and the social and economic benefits of organizing; how men and women, like his father, took risks and suffered violence for the cause. Greg says:

> Hearing some of those stories made quite an impression on a little kid . . . that benefits such as social security, minimum wage, pensions and workplace safety aren't present because of some benevolence from people at the top, be they government or corporate. They resulted from hard-fought, hard-won, no-guarantee results of average, ordinary people doing extraordinary things.

Greg was/is also significantly shaped by his experiences as a person with disabilities:

> I was born with a physical disability (scoliosis), and had numerous operations and a great deal of physical therapy as a child. I couldn't have developed any degree of physical, mental, or emotional stability without the incredible assistance from my own immediate family and others: doctors and nurses, psychologists and therapists, teachers and counselors. It was a collective effort. You know, this reality we call community is an enormously important factor in helping people either make it or not in life.

I was among the first group of physically disabled kids "mainstreamed" in the Akron public school system. It was quite an experience as teachers and counselors tried to figure out how the heck to integrate us into a "normal" setting. They didn't know how physically, mentally, or emotionally prepared we were. In some respects, they viewed us as guinea pigs and tried out different approaches. In part, we were victims, but in part, because they really didn't know what they were doing, they consulted with us and genuinely tried to take our views into account. Many of us were integrated into "normal" able-bodied classrooms and were asked: "How much was too much; are we putting too great emotional stress on you by drawing you in with all the other kids who are able bodied or not?" It was a blend between feeling like guinea pigs and feeling like respected human beings, a mixed feeling of being treated in some instances as a subject and in other instances feeling treated with dignity and respect, that your voices counted and views mattered. I think that helped me later in social change work. [One needs to] learn how to shape campaigns, write press releases, run meetings, and all those sort of technical nuts and bolts things, but social change work is also about putting yourself in someone else's shoes.

Greg's work as executive director of the NE Ohio American Friends Service Committee (AFSC) is centered mostly in a program called the Economic Justice and Empowerment Program. He explains:

AFSC is a Quaker social action organization that has been around since 1917. It began as an expression for people, not just Quakers, but also Mennonites, Brethren, and others who wanted to support this country but who did not support war and violence as a means of resolving problems. So they created an organization to provide humanitarian assistance and relieve suffering to those on both sides of World War I, which was controversial.

Since one of the basic organizing principles of the Quaker-based organization is to see good or God in every person regardless of race, nationality, religion, political affiliation, physical ability, sexual orientation, and the like, AFSC is called to provide service to all. The assistance is more than humanitarian. It's enabling skills to help people achieve self-reliance, including help to develop their own institutions and self-confidence that can carry on long after AFSC moves on.

Experiences from the war led AFSC's founders to reflect on root causes to war. There will always be wars unless we address the root causes of injustices. This realization led AFSC to begin, in both this country and abroad, very conscientious and deliberate efforts in community education, advocacy, and organizing against wars, poverty, discrimination, and exclusion but also on behalf of economic and social justice, political inclusion, and nonviolent conflict resolution. This led to the creation of offices and programs in many places across this country and in many countries of the world. AFSC was awarded the Nobel Peace Prize in 1947 for its post–World War II relief and reconstruction work, but has certainly since then continued to work in sometimes a very quiet way, sometimes in a very visible controversial way, in some forty places around this country and thirty to forty countries around the world in doing this integration of social service and social change work.

Greg works on four major projects: a campaign-financing project that is "very seriously, aggressively, and intentionally trying to change public policy, not just educate, not just persuade, but transform rules and the laws governing how campaigns are financed." He works "in support of a community organization, a grassroots group located in Uniontown, Ohio, located between Akron and Canton, that has been trying to expose the presence of an EPA designated Superfund toxic landfill. This group has, for the better part of thirty years, been educating, advocating, and organizing for a safe and permanent cleanup of this site and working to try to get significant change." He is also working on addressing the root causes and aftermath of the September 11 attacks on the World Trade Center, which invites the public to "pause and reflect on some of our own actions as a country and our domestic policy and more significantly, our foreign economic and military policies." Greg's heart, in this moment, is in the work he has been doing for the past few years challenging corporate power.

We work with activists around Ohio and, to a certain extent, across the country who have been battling private corporate power: individual companies, corporate lobby groups, or corporately friendly legislators and judges that have run roughshod over the ability of citizens to make decisions affecting their lives. Several years ago, I participated in a workshop in Ohio led by people connected to a national group called Programs on Corporation Law and Democracy (POCLAD). They were going around state by state, meeting with frustrated activists who, like themselves, have been working for years in the environmental, legal, consumer, and labor arenas battling one company at a time, one labor lawsuit at a time, one toxic dump at a time, one sweatshop at a time. POCLAD felt there wasn't enough time to deal with all the individual corporate harms, that we the people were losing more self-determination every day, that something more fundamental had to be considered. Therefore, they began questioning and examining the basic, inherent structural relationship between human persons and this human creation, the corporation, that is often bigger than any person, groups of persons, in some cases even nation-states; a legal entity which has amassed constitutional rights to govern and by doing so has trumped the rights of citizens to govern themselves. POCLAD helped us here in Ohio, as well as others in other states, come to the realization that we needed to step back from some of our single-issue fire fighting and rethink/restrategize our work and actions to be more intentional and proactive. We educate the public to help people understand how we got into this mess did not happen overnight, was not because of some cosmic forces, and was not by accident but because of an intentional effort over generations by a few who wanted to use this corporate form as a shield to rule. It's going to take the same sort of intentionality, understanding, deliberation, and collaboration to democratically govern ourselves. Hopefully, we can be more inclusive this time around. We've written a booklet, produced a documentary [http://afsc.net/economic-justice.htm], spoken and organized workshops statewide. Our message is, to whatever extent we had democracy, or still have democracy, it was due to the unique and important role of social movements, not because of top-down efforts from the politicos or corporatos. It is the work of people like ourselves. Ordinary people doing extraordinary things. We must create, yet again, a social movement—this time for inclusive democracy.

Greg considers his work to be public service, weighted more toward the end of social change. Social change is "attempting to improve the community at large, not simply in an immediate or temporary way, but in a more structural, fundamental, long-lasting way." He does his work outside of government because:

When I was in college in Ohio, I had the opportunity in study at Boston University for a semester and do an internship at the Massachusetts state planning agency. I experienced state planners discounting the views of the public. That's when I knew I didn't want to go to grad school to be an urban planner or urban administrator. I witnessed planners say, "We can't put this building there because the state representative doesn't approve, he wants it elsewhere because you know the contract is to be awarded to somebody who potentially gives them money." It was just unbelievable. I didn't want to have anything to do with that. I came back dedicated to not being a pawn of political decisions or working for an agency that would belittle public input and my own abilities. I actually felt sorry for the state planners that I was interning for because of the misuse, if not abuse, of their professional talents. I knew I had to connect with something that was more grassroots, that was not associated with government which seemed unresponsive to the public, out of control, and used by others for individual gain.

Greg thinks his work both is and is not transformational.

The flip side of working with grassroots groups that are outside of positions of power is that they are not inherently invited to be seated around the table when significant decisions are made. Yes, your voice can be more authentic, but you have no power unless you build it collectively from the ground up, and once you do, you just have to ascend these amazing hurdles before you're even recognized. Once recognized, you're criticized and you have to organize more to ascend another hurdle or another peak. If lucky enough to be still standing and those with you are still standing and haven't been bought off, burned out, or distracted, you can win a seat at the table. Even then, the elites will try to kill the momentum by granting only a small part of your demands or try to appease a part of the group, a divide-and-conquer technique.

It's just darn hard to achieve much of anything given the power that you are up against in doing this kind of work. I've come to the realization that you have to pick your struggles and see what you can realistically accomplish in the short term. The forces that we are up against are so entrenched and this issue of the breath and depth of corporate governance is so new that all we can do is set the table and begin the process. For me, it has been very instructive to study the history of social movements to see what others who have been in somewhat equivalent positions, what they have gone through, what they have struggled against, what they have been able to achieve. You know in one life span some things are possible, some aren't. That's fine. We'll just do what we can, and at the end, pass along the torch and expect others will be there to carry it. If they'll be able to harvest more fruits—that's okay, I can live with that. You have to realize that some goals may not be doable within a period of time.

Maybe we'll be surprised. Things don't always progress in equal spaces or equal units, nature doesn't work that way, and I think social change has an awful lot to learn from how the natural world works. At some point nature progresses very incrementally, but then at other points, you know, the tree falls, the hurricane or tornado happens, the tidal wave comes up. There are incremental occurrences that lead up to those changes, but then there are the sudden bursts. Nature is both incremental and sudden, and I think social change is the same. If we understand that going in and realize both what is and what is not possible in one year, one decade, one generation, then we inoculate ourselves from burning out and help others to see it's a process and we need to respect the process—the means, the way, and where it leads. The results may be something that maybe we shouldn't be concerned about because it may be simply outside our control.

Greg is sustained, nurtured, and animated by his zest for knowledge and a lifelong-learner perspective. When asked how he takes care of himself, he responded:

During a sabbatical, I studied three different types of social change. One was community organizing in this country, sort of a Saul Alinsky [1989] model. I went to Chicago where many groups exist using the Alinsky-style of community organizing. Since there was much community organizing done through church-based organizations, I spent some time meeting with people in that forum. The second of the three parts was going down South and meeting with groups started by a Quaker in North Carolina working on what are called the Listening Projects. This involved doing lengthy one-on-one interviews around a controversial issue, helping people realize that issues are not black and white, there are different shades of gray, and maybe what is needed is meeting other people to explore commonalities in the shades of gray. It was a very interesting approach. I took part in one of these issues at Camp LeJune in North Carolina, interviewing military people around the issue of conscientious objection. It was an amazing couple of days. Finally, I wanted an international experience, and I had always been fascinated by Gandhi and his work so I went to India. I spent seven weeks there visiting many Gandhian organizations. I had planned to go with a group, but that spring Rajiv Gandhi was assassinated and the trip was canceled. I went there myself and met many different people, and experienced to what extent the Gandhian model of social changed worked, was still respected and used, and was applicable to our culture and my work. Traveling and studying, respecting the sanctity of sabbatical, is of the ways I cope.

Another way I recharge myself is to realize and acknowledge that right now there are people in places like Chicago, North Carolina, India, and thousands of other places that are struggling, that are doing what I'm doing (no doubt a whole lot more effectively) and getting other people involved. When I take the time to stop, pause, and reflect, I know my work is not irrelevant or isolated. I know it because I've met some of these people, and I know there are many others doing similar work.

I'm encouraged and strengthened from studying the legal history of corporations, how citizens tried to control corporations, then lost control, then fought back, from studying the history of populism, both nationally and in Ohio, and from learning about the tremendous odds people who came before us faced without knowing where any of it would lead. When studying the legal and the corporate history of Ohio, I ran into the history of the abolitionists in Ohio—prophetic efforts among religious people and others. I also came across some of the history in Ohio that led women to advocate for suffrage, beginning at the Seneca Falls Women's Rights Convention. And again, I'm reminded of my dad being involved in the formation of the labor movement. You read and reflect on this and think, "My gosh, what people have done!" I cannot help but be unbelievably inspired and unbelievably possessed with responsibility.

We need to raise our own expectations that we can create a better world. It's our responsibility; it's our obligation. If not us, whom? If not now, when? I've also been fortunate to be around and surrounded by some amazing people who are not paid for this kind of work and give up their weekends, family time, and sometimes take vacations to work for change. It's just amazing.

In Their Words

Greg Coleridge

*What lessons would you like to share with others who want
to practice transformational public service?*

1. Ground your work in an immediate problem felt by the community(ies) or
   constituency(ies) you are working with, but connect it to broader systemic, structural issues that can only be changed if those structures or
   institutions are changed. Social service should not be an end but a means
   to social change.

2. Transformation is best created and maintained when plans for it contain
   several elements. There must be one or more ways to recruit new people
   via alternatives to the present system involving meeting one or more
   immediate needs. There must be one or more democratic structures that
   develop visions and plans that people can call their own. There must one
   or more means to communicate with constituents. And there needs to be
   an ability to apply pressure on the dominant institution(s) to bring change.

3. Seek a balance between what appear to be polar opposites. Learn to not
   only live with but accept paradoxes and contradictions: To reflect felt
   needs yet be prophetic, to build organization yet at times personally
   witness, to focus on a single activity yet connect it to everything else, to
   enable others to lead yet be prepared at key times to step out ahead, to
   be patient in building and developing groups and campaigns yet have a
   sense of urgency, to focus on the familiar yet to expose and be exposed
   to new and different strategies and tactics, to work in coalition yet at
   times go it alone organizationally, to learn from history yet carve new
   approaches, to condemn unjust and oppressive structures needing transformation yet accept as humans the people within those structures, to
   be uncompromising on one's "essential" values and strategies yet compromising on less important ones, to relish any and all "victories" yet
   see the incompleteness of them and how short-term "losses" can contain important seeds to long-term successes.

4. Don't simply focus on "bad apples" (persons, governmental entities,
   business corporations). It is critical to address institutional impediments
   to democratic and consensual self-governance. For me, this has increasingly meant focusing on the anatomy of the business corporation and
   the antidemocratic elements of the U.S. Constitution. People of privilege and property have used the vehicle of the business corporation and
   the shield of the U.S. Constitution (in particular the perversion of the Bill
   of Rights) to maintain their position of power and domination over we

the people. Needed is deliberate and disciplined learning of the evolution of the business corporation and the Constitution, rethinking our own activism, and envisioning ways that citizens can (re-)create institutions and policies that are authentically democratic—which is light years from what we have now.

5. Don't ignore the personal. As human beings, we must be open to transforming ourselves, to be more nonviolent, aware, and compassionate in our own thinking and doing. Be genuine. Admit shortcomings. Take time to reflect. Ask for help.

There is such a crying need for change: the problems, the magnitude, the severity of what we are up against is arguably as great, if not greater, than at any other moment in history given the whole environmental mess and, because of technology, our ability to screw up one another and screw up the environment. Faced with that, how can we not be involved to what extent we can without driving ourselves absolutely crazy? You just can't throw your entire psyche into it, you have to maintain some sort of healthy personal and professional balance, but how can we not do what we can to bring change? The opportunity is immense.

When I get down, what helps me recover are elements of Taoism—the whole notion of life being a paradox. Both at the same time: good and bad, hopeful and not hopeful. I understand that life is a paradox and what is required is maintenance of a balance between engagement in the work and realizing that the engagement may not necessarily lead to much. It's still important to do because it's important work to do and might make a difference, but might make absolutely no difference. This uncertainty/ambivalence/contradiction, rather than scaring me, I accept. I accept it as natural, as part of life, and so I'm not going to be terrified when something bad happens—something positive will happen that will balance it. Even in the bad, there are kernels of something very good. Every example that somebody can find, I can find the opposite.

Comment

Citizenship and Governance in Twenty-first-Century America

What does it mean to practice transformational public service? Is there anything about this historical moment that makes it ripe for rethinking approaches to public service? We believe so.

We find ourselves stymied lately when students speak of being discouraged about pursuing degrees in public administration at a time when working for the government may be the last thing they want to do. We promote the notion that "government is us," while at the same time we both say, "but, maybe not *this* particular government." Add to this the increasing costs of higher education, the vanishing student grant, and the dismal employment opportunities in our "jobless" economic recovery, and it comes as no surprise that many are just downright discouraged about practicing public service.

However, we firmly believe that transformational public service is exactly what is needed at a time in which "money talks and citizens don't." Transformational public service is an antidote to consumption-based (consumer) citizenship and the ever-increasing power of corporations and the inequities of our current economy. Transformational public service can be practiced both within traditional government organizations and within nonprofit and the other nongovernmental organizations that are springing up to fill the government gap in a time of downsizing and "businessification" of public service.

This is an especially important time to reconsider the role of public servants and ground our comments in two related places. One is the state of life in the contemporary United States; the second is the drive for reform in government and public service. Both of these take place in what some call the "postmodern condition."

Postmodernism is less a chronological epoch than a distinct social perspective. It is different from modernism, though not necessarily a step forward. Looking back over Western history, the Enlightenment arose as a reaction to the medieval worldview, roughly AD 675–1500, in which humanity was defined in relationship to the divine. The cosmos was ordered as a hierarchy, with God at the apex. Kings ruled through divine right. This religious (Christian) era represented a distinct break from paganism, in which multiple deities were worshipped and the connection to the rhythms of nature was strong. Manchester (1993) writes of this age: "The Church was indivisible, the afterlife a certainty; all knowledge was already known. *And nothing would ever change*" (p. 27; italics in original).

The Enlightenment represented illumination by the "brilliant searchlight of human scientific reason" (Hauke, 2001, p. 31). Manchester describes the coming of the Renaissance, which paved the way for the Enlightenment.

> The mighty storm was swiftly approaching, but Europeans were not only unaware of it; they were convinced that such a phenomenon could not exist. Shackled in ignorance, disciplined by fear, and sheathed in superstition, they trudged into the sixteenth century in the clumsy, hunched, pigeon-toed gait of rickets victims, their vacant faces, pocked by smallpox, turned blindly toward the future they thought they knew—gullible, pitiful innocents who were about to be swept up in the most powerful, incomprehensible, irresistible vortex since Alaric had led his Visigoths and Huns across the Alps, fallen on Rome, and extinguished the lamps of learning a thousand years before. (1992, p. 27)

Enlightenment brought faith in objective observation, measurement, and rules for experimentation—the beginnings of the scientific method. Originally, the Latin word *modernus* distinguished the Christian era from the pagan or ancient eras. During the Renaissance its meaning began to shift, and with the Enlightenment the term "modern" took on an evaluative quality, in which things modern assumed a distinctive and superior position over the religious and/or the aesthetic (Hauke, 2001).

British historian Arnold Toynbee is often credited with coining the term "postmodern" in the context of social and political history (Hauke, 2001). By this he meant the decline of Western (and Christian) influence, the demise of atomistic individualism, and the emergence of plural "narratives." Toynbee suggested the idea of a "post-Modern" age, beginning in 1875, to delineate a fourth stage of Western history after the Dark Ages (675–1075), the Middle Ages (1075–1475), and the Modern (1475–1875), although he later shifted these chronological divisions. This new era represented a dramatic rupture from the previous modern age—a middle-class, bourgeois era marked by social stability, rationalism, and progress. The postmodern age, by contrast, was characterized by wars, social turmoil, and revolution—a "time of troubles" marked by the collapse of rationalism and the ethos of the Enlightenment.

While the postmodern age may be a "time of troubles" characterized by social unrest, turmoil, and upheaval brought about by the collapse of belief systems, there are many things about this age that allow significant change and transformation. For the purposes of our analysis some of the more relevant characteristics of postmodernism include:

- *Commodification.* The economy begins to take over all sectors of society, including the government. Everything, including citizenship, becomes a perceived commodity.
- *Fragmentation.* The coherent explanations (grand narratives) offered by the modern worldview no longer cohere. Where the modern mind perceived an autonomous, self-determining individual with a secure unitary identity, the postmodern consciousness sees partiality, fragmentation, illusion, and contradiction. This leads to a fragmentation of consensus (assuming consensus ever existed) and creates a climate within which it is very difficult to do the public's business.
- *Negation.* Postmodern analysis often sounds fatalistic, nihilistic, and pessimistic. As a reflection on modernism, postmodernism focuses on the dark side of what modernism has produced: bureaucracy, technological domination, impersonality, and the destruction of nature. This negation is important, though, in revealing new possibilities.
- *Anxiety.* Continual critique and deconstruction produces great social and individual anxiety and insecurity. Hyperreflexivity brings continuous, iterative contemplation. Where is the predictability we have come to expect? What are the rules in a context where all rules are challenged?
- *Opportunity.* Along with the fragmentation of grand narratives, however, comes the opportunity not only for change, but for transformation. As society becomes more fragmented, hyperreal, and virtual, our formerly stabilizing touchstones and foundations of identity are lost. This destabilization presents tremendous opportunity for formerly marginalized groups and personal aspects (gender, race, sexual orientation) to surface and participate in the transformational process.

It is within this context of opportunity, however challenging, that the work of transformational public service is situated.

We find validations for our argument—that the time is particularly ripe for transformational public service—in the conditions of life in contemporary United States and in contemporary American public administration. The need to practice transformational public service becomes even more apparent in examining the complexities and challenges of contemporary life in this postmodern epoch and, to date, government responses to these challenges.

Life in Contemporary United States

In December 2003, the United States Congress passed the Medicare reform bill. Analyses of the bill differ (depending upon one's ideological orientation) as to who benefits and does not, but there is one point of agreement: the big winners are pharmaceutical and insurance companies. The jury is still out (and will be for years) as to the benefits of this bill for our elders. The jury is still out (and will be for years) as to how much this reform is going to cost citizens and their governments. Instead of a reform that benefits the elderly and those in need of care, the reform may be a government bailout or intervention on behalf of pharmaceutical and insurance companies. Instead of stepping in and regulating drug and insurance costs and/or opening the closed U.S. drug markets to competition from other countries, the bill follows typical neoconservative protocol and protects pharmaceutical and insurance companies from the tyranny of regulation and control.

How the bill was passed is also significant. Unprecedented voting procedures were used in the House. Most of the deliberations and committee meetings took place in closed settings. A National Public Radio story reported that there was not one Medicare beneficiary in the Senate chambers at the time of deliberation while the lobbyist room down the hall was packed full. So much crafting of the architecture of the bill was done at the last minute that the news media were, in a way, taken by surprise by the particulars of the bill. And Medicare recipients had no idea what they were getting with this reform, other than the metamessage that they were going to be better off. It was only after the bill was passed that its details filtered out to mainstream media outlets. Most found out about the details of the bill after it was too late to do anything about it. We have no option now but to live with it and see what happens.

This is one of the paradoxes of contemporary life in the United States. We have more information available to us than ever before, but we seem to be more ignorant and passive observers of policy than ever before in our history. To claim our ignorance is due to some great conspiracy would be as naïve and wrongheaded as it would be to claim our ignorance is due to our stupidity and stupor. Perhaps there is someone (or a group of someones) behind the curtain (pay no attention, Dorothy!), but probably not—that is too simplistic a premise. It is also far too simplistic to believe that we are all apathetic, lazy citizens who choose to be clueless (and feckless) about public affairs. As in most cases, there is something in the in-between. This something is what we are calling the state of life in the contemporary (postmodern) United States, situated at the confluence of social, political, and economic conditions in the United States and in the world.

And what is this life? It is a life that is organized around consumption, disempowerment, isolation, fear, and inequalities/inequities. In a postcolonial world, it could be argued that the United States is moving back toward imperialism both at home (see the USA PATRIOT Act) and abroad. Citizenship is contextualized as consumption—citizens are now tax-paying "consumers" of government services; to be a better citizen, one is exhorted to go out and buy products. We live in a culture that fears the "other" and fear keeps citizens in their place (Kristeva, 1982; Glassner, 2000). As filmmaker Michael Moore aptly illuminated in his film *Bowling for Columbine* (MGM Studios, 2002), it is not the presence of firearms that leads to excessively high murder rates in the United States, as compared with other countries—it is our fears. And these fears are played upon daily, in politics and in the media. Terrorism has exacerbated the fear of the other; our leaders trade on this fear to garner political power. Public policy is mostly made behind closed doors, without engagement of the citizens, with special interests and corporations trumping all other input.

Today the possibilities for substantial democracy and equality are significantly affected by two major phenomena: money talks and citizens don't.

Money Talks

In a corporatized, consumption-based political economy, the goal of life, it seems, is to increase one's own wealth, assets, status, and possessions. The economic boom of the 1990s was just the place within which to do so: unemployment was down, people were moved off welfare rolls, the market was booming, and most were prospering. Although we were led to believe all was well, in fact only a small percentage of the population was actually benefiting from the boom. During the 1990s the gap between the rich and the poor grew wider and the middle class shrank. In the current economic downturn, the gaps are growing even wider. In 1970, the top .01 percent of taxpayers in the United States earned seventy times as much as average taxpayers. In 1998, the top .01 percent (13,000 families) had almost as much income as the 20 million poorest and incomes 300 times that of average families (Krugman, 2002).

This transformation has happened very quickly, and it is still going on. Many believe this transformation was predicated by what Krugman calls "the Great Compression"—the substantial reduction in inequality during the New Deal and World War II—which he attributes to the creation of the middle class in the United States. This compression, however, seems hard to understand in terms of the usual theories. During World War II Franklin Roosevelt used government control over wages to compress wage gaps. But if the middle-class society that emerged from the war was an artificial creation, why did it persist for another thirty years?

In the middle of the 1980s, as economists became aware that something important was happening to the distribution of income in America, they formulated several powerful hypotheses about its causes. The "globalization" hypothesis tied America's changing income distribution to the growth of world trade, and especially the growing imports of manufactured goods from the third world. Its basic message was that blue-collar workers—the sort of people who used to make as much money as college-educated middle managers—were losing ground in the face of competition from low-wage workers in Asia. A result was stagnation or decline in the wages of ordinary people, with a growing share of national income going to the highly educated.

A second hypothesis, "skill-biased technological change," situated the cause of growing inequality not in foreign trade but in domestic innovation. The torrid pace of progress in information technology, so the story went, had increased the demand for the highly skilled and educated. And so the income distribution increasingly favored brains rather than brawn.

Another perspective claims that social norms play a role in setting limits to inequality. According to this view, the New Deal had a more profound impact on American society than even its most ardent admirers have suggested: it imposed norms of relative equality in pay that persisted for more than thirty years, creating the broadly middle-class society we came to take for granted. But those norms began to unravel in the 1970s and since then have done so at an accelerating pace.

In the 1960s, America's great corporations behaved more like socialist republics than like cutthroat capitalist enterprises. Top executives behaved more like public-spirited bureaucrats than like captains of industry. John Kenneth Galbraith offered a description of executive behavior in his 1967 book *The New Industrial State* that seems foreign today. He described management as constrained, not ruthlessly out to reward itself, and a bastion of group decision making that ensures that actions and thoughts are known to all and that unspoken codes ban greed and avarice. Indeed, he argued, the very base of capitalism depended upon the good works of managers, encouraging a high standard of corporate and personal honesty.

Thirty-five years later, a cover article in *Fortune Magazine* is titled "You Bought. They Sold" (2002). "All over corporate America," reads the blurb, "top execs were cashing in stocks even as their companies were tanking. Who was left holding the bag? You."

The phenomenal increases in the gap between the rich and the poor, the shrinking middle class (and its inevitable disempowerment as a result), and the rising power and avarice of corporations have led to a situation that is unprecedented in U.S. history. We have, historically, been a country of active citizenship and active dissent. Historical accounts of citizenship and democracy in the United States abound with examples of active citizenship, starting with the founding of our country and continuing through the social movements of the twentieth century. It is part of our common lore that Alexis de Tocqueville, a French aristocrat visiting the United States in the 1830s and author of *Democracy in America,* found a place animated by a deep democratic and egalitarian spirit. Yes, there were elites, but life was, according to Tocqueville, apparently much more influenced by association and community than it was by material well-being. (Also, keep in mind that Tocqueville chose to ignore slavery and the limitations to political life for women and people of color.)

Tocqueville, somehow, occupied an in-between of "right" and "left" views: his experiences in the United States made him both a critic of addiction to material well-being and an apostle of civic engagement as well as a critic of big government and doctrinaire egalitarianism (Kimball, 2000). Nonetheless, his experiences in the United States led him to believe that a deeply engaged populace is essential for democratic freedom and liberty.

Since Tocqueville, the United States has been considered "exceptional." Tocqueville intended this phrase to reflect his observation that the United States is qualitatively different from other western societies in that it developed under a separate set of assumptions, organizing principles, and hence, political and religious institutions (Lipset & Marks, 2000). Other scholars and observers have noted that America's exceptionalism has produced far weaker protections for the nonwealthy, despite periods of reform that were specifically focused on the average citizen, including Jacksonian democracy, the Populist movement, trade unionists, and the progressives.

American exceptionalism resulted in weaker structural protections for the average citizen primarily because it drew on the profound liberalism and individualism inherent in the American worldview. Even American radicals were more sympathetic to libertarianism than their European counterparts. Unlike movements such as Scandinavian social democracy or Fabian bureaucratic socialism in England, American radicalism maintained an inherent suspicion of centralized powers of authority, especially those of the government. Furthermore, America's lack of a historical class structure encouraged a collective vision of, and belief in, social mobility. Our vast amount of available territory enabled individual land ownership for nearly everyone who wanted it (and was willing to take it away from the indigenous dwellers). American exceptionalism simultaneously reinforced our sense of community and our sense of individualism, especially through property ownership (Lipset & Marks, 2000).

American exceptionalism and the economic forces of the last century create conditions under which when "money talks," particularly when connected with greed, citizens don't. The next section addresses the latter.

Citizens Don't Talk

Concerns about the condition of America's civic climate are growing. Despite continued adherence to our beliefs in constitutional democracy, equal opportunity, and social freedom, citizens' faith in the system that presumably enables and protects these beliefs is declining sharply. Beyond that, the percentage of Americans who believe that the country's moral condition is waning has increased (Galston, 2002). Political analysts bemoan the lack of consensus in American politics and policy; apparently, we are deeply divided, even when we share a basic concern about "how things are going" in our country and in the world. While unity sounds appealing, we must also remember that its appearance is often created through the suppression of dissenting voices.

While it is not often readily apparent, active citizenship is related to the political economy of a state. According to classical Marxist thought, one of the key elements of democratic citizenship—the idea of equality—is impossible in an economy where the ownership of the means of production is separate from those who produce (the workers). In a postcapitalist, corporatized, consumption-based economy where our place in the world is determined by the goods we own or *have* and not by who we *are* apart from our possessions, the possibilities for active citizenship are even more constrained. There are few places for active citizenship (including a concern for the common good) in a political economy driven by individual wants and needs.

Conventional wisdom assumes, as David Morris (1999, p. 24) notes: "bigger is better, that separating the producer from the consumer, the banker from the depositor, the worker from the owner, the government from its citizens is a necessary requirement for achieving a prosperous economy and a healthy society." Morris posits that "seeing with new eyes" (à la T.S. Eliot's stanza from the "Four Quartets," reprinted at the end of this book) requires that we unpack or deconstruct the assumptions that lie under our quest for progress, no matter what the cost.

Progress has served, but it has also cost us. The costs to the environment are well known and well documented in the alternative and, increasingly, mainstream literature. However, there are other significant costs as well to unquestioned progress. Many of these costs are relational. As we get further away from a political economy that requires people to work and interact together to meet their daily needs, we dilute and dull our relational capacities.

In a consumption-based economy, our well-being is measured by what we have (what Eric Fromm, 1979, calls "having") versus what we are (or "being"). Over time

> it has been our relationship to things which has threatened our relationships to each other as human beings. In the process of having more and more material things we come to treat each other as things. The "having" mode of existence dominates the "being" mode of existence. The consumer has replaced the creative producer as the goal of human existence, and in that process having has tended to squeeze out being. The acquisition of goods for reasons of status, as encouraged through advertising and consumerism, and for power over others characterizes the having mode. [Alternatively] being is related to internal self-development that takes place through relationship with other human beings." (Twine, 1994, pp. 176–77)

Exchange, market-based relationships promote the growth of a universalistic culture and contribute to the emergence of consumption-based individualism by emphasizing the autonomy of the consumer. Late twentieth-century consumption-based capitalism exacerbated the conditions that subtract from citizenship: inequalities of income, status, and prestige in the market and workplace; an excessive focus on the economic self; and a lack of "we thinking" (Barber, 1984). Where citizens are able to achieve greater equality, control over the means of production, and greater democracy, they "necessarily interfere with the workings of profit and accumulation in the economic system" (Turner, 1986, p. 24). When active citizenship interferes with the workings of profit and accumulation, those who desire profit and accumulation will work to limit citizen engagement. As active citizenship has declined in the United States, the powers of corporations and other special interests have increased (and vice versa).

Furthermore, in contemporary culture, we tend to take our identity not from our membership in a nation-state, but rather from our membership in a consumption relationship to a corporation. We identify ourselves as citizens of these corporate-nations by wearing their symbols. One may be more a member of a Nike nation (displaying the "swish" on one's ball cap and other clothing) than one is a member of a nation-state. Although this abated a bit with patriotism after September 11, 2001, we are now called upon to show our "allegiance to our nation" by purchasing products that are emblems for patriotism. After September 11, 2001, George W. Bush called us to show our citizenship not by becoming more active, engaged citizens but by shopping. And we complied.

A central premise of citizenship defined by consumption with a corporate-nation is that there are relatively few communal aspects of one's belonging and almost no responsibilities attached to one's membership. Citizens of corporate-nations are not citizens in the truest sense of the word. We do not have responsibilities to a community or to other citizens; we only have responsibilities to and for ourselves and, perhaps, our families.

Corporate citizenship exacerbates the growing divides between people and our fear of, and competition with, others. Fear is a powerful motivator. A fearful populace is a compliant populace. A fearful populace is not likely to rise up against those in power. Indeed, a fearful populace is not likely even to want to talk about power and undermine those who do by labeling them dissenters. A fearful populace is likely to keep to themselves, take care of themselves, and minimize contacts with strangers and others (including neighbors). A fearful population assuages its fears through consumption; compliant consumers are good consumers (Glassner, 2000). Good consumers are not necessarily good citizens.

Convincing people they are best served by gating their communities, staying in their homes, keeping to themselves, and avoiding their neighbors makes for a population that gets out of the way when one wants to get something done. We have created a citizenry that does not talk to each other or to decision makers. Our exceptionalism, as seen by Tocqueville, has, as he predicted, led to a nation that is a mere shadow of its former self with regard to community and citizenship.

Kevin Phillips (2003) posits that if we do not renew democracy, increasing wealth for some is apt to lead to a less democratic regime. As Krugman (2002, p. 142) states:

> Even if the forms of democracy remain, they may become meaningless. It's all too easy to see how we may become a country in which the big rewards are reserved for people with the right connections; in which ordinary people see little hope of advancement; in which political involvement seems pointless, because in the end the interests of the elite always get served.

To be fair, there are many movements on the margins and at the center of public policy that seek to renew and deepen democracy. Not all citizens and special interests groups are silenced by the loud voices of money talking. Indeed, it could be argued that we are experiencing a surge in activism, spawned by war, burgeoning deficits, an economic downturn, and countless setbacks in environmental and social policy. Governments and citizens across the country are beginning to work more closely together. Citizens are calling for reform in government, for greater accountability and transparency. They want governments to be more effective. They want government to work better. When government does not work well, citizen activists work to promote change. Public service does need reform. Yet, our response has been limited.

Public Service Needs Reform

There is no doubt that government needs reform with respect to efficiency, effectiveness, and citizen engagement. There have been many recent movements to increase citizen involvement and engagement, particularly in local-level activities. Indeed, one cannot pick up a publication addressing public administration or public service and not find articles referencing effective movements to engage citizens in their governments. Still, the majority of the reform work being done in the fields of public administration and public policy—in scholarship and in practice—is on *how* we administer to improve accountability, efficiency, and effectiveness in our work. This makes sense as we are, after all, about administering. When calls for reform are made, we turn toward that which we know best: how to administer.

Still, many of these reform movements may be off target. The contemporary shortcomings of American public administration happen around failures in policy and administrative practices that were designed in the tradition of classical liberalism. Models (solutions) of new governance are responses to limitations of democracies built in the classical liberalism tradition, particularly limitations in American democracy.

According to Charles Heying (1999), classical liberalism is a uniquely modern political solution, designed to address problems of premodern times (but, not necessarily, of postmodern times). This is best recognized in the primary tenets of classical liberalism: rejection of absolute power; resistance to other sources of power (including the tyranny of the majority); and the belief that society exists to serve individuals, therefore political solutions are designed to protect individuals from interference from both the state and others. As a result, classical liberalism magnifies personal property and minimizes the ability of authorities to limit individual rights. This puts government at the periphery and nongovernment institutions, particularly the market, at the center. While some may argue that classical liberalism is weak in this moment and government is very much over determining our individual lives (see, for example, Spicer, 2004; Fox, 2003), a quasi-government is currently in power. Businesses and their interests reign.

Although classical liberalism ostensibly freed us from the dark ages of pre–Enlightenment politics, it also "unlocked our capacity to create worlds of our own choosing and endowed ourselves with inalienable rights. [T]he very success of our liberation has set us adrift. We find ourselves alone, alienated, cut loose from the certainties of place, tradition, and communal solidarity" (Heying, 1999, p. 39).

In the midst of this lonely place, in the mainstream of contemporary American public administration, one finds mostly private (individualized) solutions to our contemporary dilemmas. Reform movements such as New Public Management, reinvention and performance management, and performance/outcome measurement are refinements and revisions of the market and management solutions applied in the past. As movements to perfect the science of administration, these responses make sense in that they track very closely to classical liberalism—they do not threaten our root values and assumptions.

Responses that are fundamentally private miss the point that we need less emphasis on the private individual and more emphasis on the public collective or public good. We do not need to make government more individualistic, more corporatized, and more disconnected from the people. We do not need to make government more administrative. We need to make our governments more democratic. To paraphrase Audre Lorde, we cannot remake the master's house using the master's tools. We must use different tools.

What is the role of public administration in this context? Is it only to focus on the implementation of policy (the old founding dichotomy)? If so, our emphasis is rightly placed on perfecting the techniques of administering, as the many people practicing and theorizing in mainstream public administration are doing today. It is naïve and ignorant to deny that we need to improve the functioning of government to make it more responsive and more effective. However, focusing the lens only on technique narrows our scope to such a degree that we might believe we need not pay attention to the normative questions involved in our work—it is not just *how* we administer but, equally important, *why* we administer and *who* benefits.

The role of contemporary public administration, in our view, is to work to find the different tools needed to remake public life such that it is more democratic and less privatistic. These tools need to address the central tension of modernity, according to Heying (1999, p. 43) by "preserving the advantages of liberalism with its emphasis on human rights, universal tolerance, and free association, while attempting to revive a type of communal solidarity that is similar, yet different from, that found in traditional societies and totalitarian regimes, . . . an alternative way that hopes to save liberalism from its own excesses."

In addressing the excesses of liberalism, the trick is not to discard the advantages in an attempt to address the shortcomings. We do need to focus on improvement such that public services meet the needs of the people (effectiveness), using resources in an appropriate manner (efficiency). But to focus only on this is shortsighted. Effectiveness in what we already do and efficiency in doing it is not enough. We must transform.

Story

Transforming Citizenship and Governance

Claire Mostel
Team Metro Citizens Academy Coordinator
Miami-Dade County, Florida

Claire Mostel considers herself to be "a child of the 60s." In college, she found public administration as a field of study—the work coupled well with her activist background. After a stint with Miami-Dade County's Clerk of Courts, she took her current position with Team Metro in 1995. Miami-Dade County includes thirty-four municipalities, cities, and townships as well as unincorporated territory.

> It was my vision and goal of working in government or public service to interact directly with people, help people with whatever problems they may have with government or in their daily lives on a more personal basis rather than pushing papers behind some desk where you never see anybody. During the 1960s, I was very antigovernment, very anti-everything. However, I realized that it is great to disagree and point out the problems/room for improvement, but you have to do more than that. You have to get out and make those changes or help facilitate those changes. I wanted to be in a position to have that opportunity.

For Claire, being a change agent means being a link between the problem and the people who want to see a different way of doing things but are unaware of how to go about doing it, do not have the proper resources, or want someone else to do it. She wanted to facilitate changes and improvements or offer ways to do so, which is why she developed and implemented the Citizens Academy.

The Citizens Academy is a twelve-week program that educates citizens in government services in order to empower them to be change agents in their communities. Claire's department provides outreach services in addition to residential and commercial code enforcement. Her former department director,

In Their Words

Claire Mostel

*What would you like to tell others about what it is like
to do the work you do?*

Every day I have the opportunity to make a difference in my community. I also have the chance to meet and interact with a diverse group of people and hear different perspectives. I have the opportunity to change public perception of government in general, and of local government staff in particular. In addition, I get a lot of abusive phone calls and in-person encounters that can really get me down and make me wonder why I stay in government, particularly outreach services; then five minutes later, I'll help someone resolve a problem and that makes it all worthwhile. As the Team Metro Citizens Academy coordinator, I have the chance to interact with residents from all over the county. During the course of the twelve-week program, the message of personal and communal responsibility is emphasized repeatedly. It is amazing to witness the transformation of the "students'" perception of county staff and themselves—how appreciative they are that county staff takes the time to interact with them and actually listen to their concerns, and respond to them one-on-one. At some point in the semester, the realization hits them that education and knowledge is power—and citizens have so much power if they use it correctly. I usually drive home from the classes on such a "high" that it takes quite some time to unwind when I get home. If you believe in our system of government, while recognizing that there's always room for improvement, if you are passionate about citizen participation and get satisfaction from making a difference, then this job is for you!

Debbie Curtin, was the kind of leader who let her staff run with good ideas. As such, she was a strong mentor for Claire.

Claire got the idea for the academy after a series of events.

Residents at the homeowners' meetings were complaining that they got a civil citation for a code violation, but felt it was not fair, that they are getting citations for things they don't know are violations. Recognizing that this county has over two million people, and covers over 2,000 square miles, you can imagine that our ordinance book is quite huge. There's no realistic way that people are going to know every violation, every ordinance that exists on the books, just like they don't know all the services that are available to them. I talked with Debbie and I said "Gee, you know, we need to find a way to get this information out there, outside the traditional sources that we already use, and to educate our residents. We want them to be involved in their government, we want them to be participants, we don't want them to just be recipients." I knew there were other similar type programs throughout the country including the cities of Hollywood and Cocoa Beach, Florida, so Debbie said, "Draft me a proposal," and I did.

The proposal was to run the program like a university on a trimester schedule: two classes run concurrently each semester, one in the north end and one in the south end of the county. We have nine Team Metro regional offices throughout our county. Each Team Metro office hosts a class for the whole semester and provides clerical and outreach support. The academy began as an eight-week program with approximately twelve county departments participating. That was in April 2000. Now the program is twelve weeks and we have seventeen participating departments. I recruited the first twelve departments—the other departments contacted us after they heard of the success with the program. The classes are limited to twenty students. I want the residents to be able to interact with each other because even though they are in a somewhat similar community area, they come from different developments and different types of homes—some are single-family homes, some live in condominiums, some are multifamily dwellings. We want to encourage interaction, first of all, between the students so they can see what is going on in other communities. Maybe they have a similar situation or problem and they can see how someone else addressed that issue or maybe didn't address it, and also to build a feeling of community. So many of us think "my community stops at the end of my development or in my section of town," not realizing that crime and poverty and lack of services and all those things that we try to improve don't know jurisdictional boundaries. We want to encourage and enlarge the sense of community. The other reason to keep it small is to allow each student the opportunity to ask as many questions as possible—the classes are very unstructured, and they just throw questions at the presenters in the middle of a sentence—a free for all. There were twenty-seven students in one of the classes last semester and not only was it unmanageable, the high number of questions cut into the allotted presentation time. If there were more students, everyone would not have an equal chance to participate. The third reason I keep it small is that I want to encourage interaction between the students and county staff. One of the goals of the academy is to improve the public perception of county staff because they think we are all lazy, worthless, "sleep in cars in parks," etc.

The Citizens Academy focuses on government services that are "quality of life" services (police, safety, public works, parks and recreation, transit, environmental resources, etc.). Claire does this work in addition to her "day job": "this is not part of my job description." Her "day job" is to manage the outreach services of a decentralized county services office, "like mini-town halls bringing government to the people so to speak. That is, before I change in a telephone booth and go to the academy."

I go to all the classes. Once in a while, I teach a Team Metro class, but it's more quality control than anything else. I facilitate the classes to make sure that the interaction between the students and the staff goes smoothly. I sort of act as a link and also build up goodwill because they get used to seeing me every week. One of the successes of Team Metro is that people know that when they call this (or any Team Metro) office, if they want to talk to a supervisor or an outreach person, I am always going to be here, so to speak. I may be out of the office at that time but they know they can leave a message and I will return their call or one of my staff will always be there to answer their questions. I put the face on government by going to all the academy sessions; it builds the relationship with the residents. They really want to know that somebody gives a damn and is really going to come to them; when you are dealing with a government this size, people feel they are not getting enough bang for their buck, that our county government is too large, that we don't have enough people to address their immediate concerns. I go to all these classes to let them know that yes, we do care and we are here for them and we will do our best to try and right whatever wrongs they feel exist. I also tell them there are going to be times I can't do what you want me to do. I do not believe in giving unrealistic expectations and sometimes some higher-ups will say, "Don't say that." I'm not going to go and compound a problem by promising something that I know damn well we can't do.

The first night of the program we have a mini civics class and talk about our local government. It's amazing how many people are uninformed about their local government and the responsibilities of county officials. We explain why we do the things that we do, why we don't do some of the things they want us to do, and discuss concepts like due process and the Sunshine Law. Most people don't even know what due process is, and don't want to know until it affects them. I try to explain to them that if we don't do some things there's usually a very logical reason for it (budget constraints, legislative constraints, etc.), and I have to explain to them that state takes priority over local, federal takes priority over state, etc. We also try to emphasize to them they have a responsibility as citizens to not just sit back and expect government to do everything for them, they have a responsibility to make us accountable to them and also to understand that county staff does not make policy—we implement policy—and, instead of taking out their frustrations on someone who has no authority to do anything, to go to the appropriate places. I don't want them to spin their wheels; they vent their frustrations at levels that can't make a difference and we try to help them get to the right area.

Claire's experiences with the Citizens Academy have been transformational, for the government, for the lives of the participants, for herself, and for the communities.

It has been truly an amazing experience to interact with the people—residents and other county staff. One of the things I do the first night of class is an icebreaker where I ask them to list three things they would like to change about their local government. It's amazing that no matter how diverse the groups are, they all want the same things; everyone thinks we're so different from everybody else, but we all have the same concerns. The change of the students' perception from the beginning of the semester to the end is unbelievable and very positive. We've had students ranging in age from twenties to eighties. Many of our graduates have joined task forces, volunteered in our offices and done other work as a result of their participation in the academy. One of the best experiences we had involved three Haitian students in a class that ended up joining forces and forming a corporation to help the Haitian community here. The group has been very successful and has invited staff to attend their functions.

Claire describes herself as very passionate.

If I believe in something, I'm very passionate about it. When I was younger it got me in trouble because I would say whatever popped in my head. I had to learn to channel that in a way that would have a more positive outcome. When I was young if somebody used a racial slur against someone else, I would go crazy, you know, and say all kinds of negative things that would turn off that person. As I got older, I realized that when you react like that, you feed into the negativity that's already there and you don't co-opt that person, you push them farther away. I learned that there were other ways to handle things and you can still maintain that level of passion.

I have a really strong belief in our form of government. It's not perfect and there's plenty of room for change, but I want to be part of that change. I'm passionate about taking control of our government because I believe in the concept that government is us. I think that's an expression that I've used before I even read your book when I talked to civics classes. I asked them, "Okay, who can tell me what government is?" They all raise their hands and say "Oh, the president, Senate, House." I say, "No, government is us, we are government." We just don't know it. I feel that we are either going to take an active role in our communities and our governments or we should stop complaining. I'm a pacifist, but I also realize that war is a natural part of life and we're always going to have war of some type, whether it's a traditional war or nuclear war, wars between gangs, that's just part of life. I may not want to fight because I don't believe in killing, but somebody's going to have to do it. As I matured, I realized that you can march in the streets, but throwing things, breaking windows, taking over classrooms or businesses doesn't really change anything. It might bring your cause to the forefront, which I believe happened in the antiwar movement, but where do you go next? You can stay an outsider and not really have a chance to make changes or you can work within the system, try to right the things you think are wrong, change the things that you think need to be changed or at least open the door to make those changes.

Claire speaks to the challenges of working for transformational change inside of government.

There are times I have to do things that are not unethical or illegal, but just upper management's style might be different than mine. I may want to do something that I think will be for the better, but I may not always be able to do that. In terms of what I do every day, I'm very up front with the people at Citizens Academy (and the office). One of the first things I tell them the first night is I'm not here to tell you that your local government is perfect and doesn't make mistakes. We do, there's plenty of room for improvement, but we can't do it ourselves. I don't believe in compromising my values or ethics for the good of the organization in terms of being deceitful or unrealistic because, in the end, it's going to come back and bite me on the butt. I don't think that the average citizen realizes how much potential power they possess or how much they give up by not participating in, at least, local government. I think it makes me unpopular to be doing this work. I don't know if I'm dangerous because I'm really a small fish in a huge pond. I do know that I have a responsibility to behave professionally, and I'm a representative of my department and my county. I want to tell our residents about all the good things that our county government does (we do plenty of good things) and sometimes I want to shake them and say your expectations are unrealistic.

Claire needs support from her leaders and her colleagues, although she often runs up against resistance from both.

If I didn't have the support of Debbie Curtin, my previous department director, the Citizens Academy would never have taken off. I was very fortunate to have the type of department director that let me work with an idea, gave me room to sink or swim, and gave me as many resources as possible to succeed. My immediate manager, Robert Santos-Alborna, was also extremely supportive by allowing me the time I needed during the day to work on the academy, even though it took time from other assignments. Debbie and Robert recognized the importance of the program and the benefits for our residents and the county and gave me the freedom and support needed to move the academy forward. However, I had many people at all levels say, "It's never going to work," and resist the idea of participation in the academy. Fortunately, our county manager at the time, Merrett Stierheim, instructed the initial departments that they "would participate and cooperate," which gave legitimacy to the program. He attended the opening night and the graduation night of the academy and was very supportive during his tenure. The Citizens Academy is in its fourth year and all of the original departments (and most of the original presenters) are still with the program. Their eventual enthusiasm has been a large factor in the success of the academy. In the fall of 2003, we started the academy with one of the county's magnet high schools. But I found that one of the problems I've had with coworkers, colleagues throughout the years, is that they really don't care about what they do and they are just sort of going through the motions. When you show that you really care, they think you are nuts—like "Why do you care what these people think, why do you care what they do, why do you care what happens?" Well, I do care. That's why I made a conscious decision to come from the private sector to the public sector, because it was something I truly believe in. So I just think it makes me unpopular.

I think people who work in public service are caretakers. I will tell you that I don't like the term public servants because to me it implies servitude and it implies that we are not part of the public. We are. I pay taxes, you pay taxes. I feel I have an obligation to behave in a professional manner according to my position for my department and for my county government, but I also have an obligation to my sense of ethics and morals and what's right and wrong and what I think I'm supposed to be here doing and I will do that—I will stretch both boundaries as much as I can get away with. This is not exactly a servitude attitude.

Whoever said knowledge is the key was right on the money. If you don't know, you can't do. Knowledge empowers people so much. But, that's another word I don't always like: empowerment. Sometimes we talk about empowering citizens. It's almost like we're giving them something as a present when the truth is that the power should already be there/is already there. They already have these rights. This is their government. I am a caretaker of our local government, not a servant. I have an obligation to provide the best service possible and provide information to everybody, not just people I think should have it or a select group that I want to have it because they are going to do what I want them to do. I want to be able to take care of the things that people want but they don't want to deal with. I think public service is caring about our community, the people who make up those communities; in the line of work that I do, if you don't have a thick skin and you don't care about those communities, you are in the wrong line of work. Our system leaves the door open for change if you want to walk through it, and I want to walk through it. I want to be part of the change; I want to be part of good, positive things that we can do both locally, state and federal. I want people to get involved. I want to show them here you can do this, you know you need to know a little bit more about what's going on.

In Their Words

Claire Mostel

What lessons would you like to share with others who want to practice transformational public service?

Change can be slow and painful. I always tell people that our local government didn't get the way it is overnight, and it won't change or improve overnight. Nor can government make things better by itself. Turnaround is dependent on desire and public-private-citizen partnership. It is important to recognize that many of the players have personal agendas and you have to be able to work within and around those agendas. In order to be effective, you have to stay current on local issues and neighborhood areas of concern. Management support from the top down is absolutely necessary; if your boss doesn't buy into the program or concept, you are dead in the water. I was very fortunate to have both a progressive and supportive department director and immediate manager when creating and implementing the Citizens Academy. Unfortunately, sometimes our own colleagues are not supportive and can be stumbling blocks in the path towards transformation. Change agents have to be able to listen and really "hear" what citizens are saying and must be open to opinions and ideas that "stretch" the bureaucratic structure that surround us. Remember, the old-school ties that bind us from being able to practice transformational public service also frustrate our citizens. Sometimes, when I am trying to explain a policy to an irate citizen, I listen to myself and think how ridiculous it sounds—no wonder there are so many irate citizens! Have realistic expectations; those who want to practice transformational public service are passionate about what they do—finding out that you may be restricted in options, or may have to take the long way to accomplish your goals can dampen enthusiasm. Persistence is a necessary trait!

Sometimes I'm so damn tired because I work at least two nights a week, in addition to my regular day job. I get home sometimes and I am so damn tired that I can't see straight and I wonder why I am doing this. But then, I will get a call from somebody thanking me for hooking them up with somebody or for helping their group do something and it's like that's it. The satisfaction is unbelievable.

Part II

Theory and Practice

Theory-Informed Practice and Practice-Informed Theory

Evelyn Brom and Sheila Hargesheimer
Human Services Department
Domestic and Sexual Violence Prevention Office
City of Seattle, Washington

> *You must be the change you wish to see in the world.*
> —Mahatma Gandhi

Evelyn Brom and Sheila Hargesheimer share office space on the thirteenth floor of the Alaska Building in downtown Seattle. The Alaska Building is adjacent to the Pioneer Square district, a section of downtown Seattle that draws large numbers of both tourists and the homeless. We met in Sheila and Evelyn's office, a physical space with an open environment that reflects their approach of how they work. Sheila is the director of the Domestic and Sexual Violence Prevention Office of the City of Seattle. Evelyn is a senior planning and development specialist in the Domestic and Sexual Violence Prevention Office. Evelyn is an alumna of the graduate program in public administration at The Evergreen State College in Olympia, Washington.

Both Sheila and Evelyn came of age in the late 1960s and early 1970s, a time when the women's movement, the black power movement, and the anti-war movement were organized and actively and successfully challenging power structures. Participating in these movements educated them about important theories. They developed skills in leading from the inside out, in public speaking, and in political organizing. During those times they were steeped in critical thinking processes they have carried with them in their work in government today.

Both Sheila and Evelyn have lived experiences that led them to pay attention to oppression and to connect oppression to political and social realities.

In Their Words

Evelyn Brom

*What would you like to tell others about what it is like
to do the work you do?*

I work in a large department in local government, in a small office with six staff called the Domestic and Sexual Violence Prevention Office. Our mission: In partnership with communities, we provide leadership and direction to city government to create communities free of domestic and sexual violence. We believe that only in a community where all members share and practice beliefs that create justice and liberty from oppression will women be free of violence in their lives [from a DSVPO brochure].

The work I do is about social justice. I have been doing work in public organizations long enough now to know that it makes a difference. The work we do shapes public policy and creates fiscal policy. This work takes a system-wide approach, fosters coordination, collaboration, and partnerships, builds on and enhances existing efforts, and incorporates research and promising practices.

Public service is a vehicle for improving our society. This work we do is social change work and requires staying committed to core life values (justice, integrity). This work challenges systems from within government. This work is about community building, improving relationships, effective collaboration, and teamwork.

In doing this work it is important we model authentic, effective leadership and base decision making and problem solving in our lived experiences as women.

Working against violence against women goes beyond single-issue politics. The work we do recognizes intersections of oppressions and incorporates work against racism, homophobia, and poverty. The work we do focuses on reforming government institutions, adapting bureaucracy for greater accessibility, being attentive to institutional, hierarchical, and white privilege, and sharing resources.

To do the work I do is many things. Because I view myself as an activist in government, the work I do is about changing the way we do the work (starting from within the office and addressing hierarchy), incorporating both more voices and more diversity in those voices.

To quote an adage from the second wave of the feminist movement, Evelyn and Sheila came to an embodied understanding that the "personal is the political" through situating their personal, lived experiences within a political perspective. As such, their eyes were opened to what is typically unspoken in our society (their own experiences with violence and gender-based exploitation and the experiences of their sisters, their childhood friends, their mothers, and mothers in their communities)—hidden experiences not named and therefore nonexistent. However these experiences were real and where they lived was in women's bodies, heads, and hearts. When one names them, one begins to analyze and then begins speaking the truth about the power systems within which we live.

For Evelyn, this lived experience was her own rape and multiple close, personal contacts with violence against women, affecting both her and her family members and friends. It led to Evelyn's realization of the prevalence of men's violence against women in our society and the silence of society on the issue. Sheila's lived experience was a childhood of scarcity. As one of the poor of the poor, she felt the scarcity as a child and now realizes that the majority of those in her county were poor, rather than only a few families as she first thought.

Evelyn's recognition of the high prevalence of violence against women and Sheila's recognition that class and gender oppression is experienced by many allowed them both to place their individual experiences in the larger social, political, and economic contexts. This is no small feat; oppression works best when the oppressed believe their experiences are not shared by others. Evelyn and Sheila both talked about "appreciating" their experiences for what they gained and the power that accompanies situating your personal experience in a political context.

> What is transforming is the politicizing of your personal experiences, especially painful and dehumanizing personal experiences. This is the first step toward activism and begins to address immobilizing, internalized oppression. Until you do this, you believe what happened is your fault, the locus of the problem is in you, and that you are inadequate. On top of this are the societal messages reinforcing this sense of inadequacy. The first step toward becoming active is recognizing that there are structural causes that limit possibilities, offer fewer opportunities, and affect your ability to conceive of possibilities, to dream, and to conceive of something bigger for yourself. These messages are socially and politically structured.

As Sheila said, "When you are able to look at your own and others' experiences in this way, all of a sudden it is something that you own and it is something that is yours. You are the one that is defining what the impact is—not it."

Evelyn's personal experiences with violence against women were crucial in the development of her activism.

> Activism against rape started receiving federal funding in the early 1970s, which is when I was raped. I ended up getting a job through government

funding, doing work beyond volunteering on the rape crisis line. Although my work was still about healing and understanding, it was increasingly becoming about activism and political change. This was an important time in my political development and for becoming an activist in government.

When asked how they bridged the gap between the personal and the political, both spoke of the importance of joining a social movement or activist organization. The movements allowed them to politicize their experiences and situate them in a larger context, educated them theoretically and pragmatically, and gave them a site for resistance.

Sheila says, "The social movements allowed me to bridge the personal and the political. Once you place your personal experiences of misogyny, racism, and classism within a political framework you have courage and motivation to look deeper and farther."

For Evelyn, her work in social movements provided more than a theoretical and systemic frame within which to place her personal experiences.

More importantly, for me, was that women's ways of organizing around this activist work showed a different way of doing things: a way that valued involvement, that flattened hierarchy, that had many voices and respect for process, experiences, and the personal. This participatory democratic organizing within the women's movement provided evidence to me that there are other and more inclusive ways to structure ourselves, to do our work, to lead, and to be governed.

According to Sheila, situating one's lived experience in a broader context is a critical step in one's personal development as an activist.

When the theory and the philosophy relate to what people are feeling in their hearts—what is authentic to them and their own authentic truth—and moves them to action, the theory, then, is a living thing generating your creativity. Ideas begin to live when you put them into practice and then the practice informs the theory. This dynamic is the core dynamic of social change: a living dynamic, always in process. This is where the creativity lives. Without this dynamic, ideas remain static. What sustained me and kept me was my own study—it really was ideas. Even now if I start feeling discouraged or I'm thinking I want to do something else, ideas keep me sane.

Sheila was very much influenced by her family's poverty. She talks about the centrality of her mother in her life. Her mother's circumstances and how she coped and lived greatly influenced Sheila. Her mother's coping mechanisms were not conformity to the rigid moral constraints of a small, southern, rural community. Rather, they pushed the limits of those confines. Her mother did not have theory for her lived experience, what she had was a deep unconditional love for her children.

> When the constraints of this environment came into conflict with what her children needed physically, emotionally, and spiritually she intuitively resisted. We learned from her that you did not have to go along, you could resist. When women connect theory with change that will improve the lives of their children and, in many instances, save the lives of their children, there exists a source of incredible power to fundamentally change the way we are in the world. Connecting women's need for change to theories that change the ways of the world is another dimension of power. It transcends and transforms qualitatively, not just quantitatively. This type of power has the potential to move us closer to our humanity. Perhaps it is the only thing that can move us closer to humanity because it is born and sustained by love. What I witnessed is the power that love has in the worst of circumstances.

Both Sheila and Evelyn believe what they bring to their work is a commitment to do it differently—to structure the work differently.

> We bring experience and knowledge to this small organization in local government. What we are trying to do that is transformational about this work is *how* we work. We are trying to apply our knowledge and experience of oppression and the practice of creating and sustaining nonhierarchical ways of doing the work learned in feminist organizations to highly bureaucratic, hierarchical structures. By functioning this way as much as possible, we challenge traditional structures. Everyone's voices and experiences and beliefs are heard, counted, valued, and incorporated. Everybody, regardless of position, race, and class, brings their voices to the work and this brings a high level of quality to the work. You have to work in this way for the dynamic between theory and practice to be real. You cannot have some people with the theory and the power to conceptualize and others being directed to implement your ideas and theories as the doers. You cannot separate conceptualization and execution. You cannot separate theory and practice. When you separate people by theory and practice (people that think and people that do), creativity is lost as is the interchange between theory and practice necessary for both the advancement of knowledge and social change. Furthermore, when theory and practice are separated in bureaucratic, hierarchical organizations you create an imbalance of power between those who have the ideas and direct others to do them. This is one way power imbalances are recreated [or reified] on a daily basis. Separating theory and practice, therefore, leads not only to lower quality work, it also reinforces power imbalances. This may be part of the

contempt for process we hear in city government. Giving over to the process of not separating ideas and practice can undermine the power of the person/s with institutional control over the ideas.

Separating theory and practice leads to theoreticians who are not informed by practice, making their work flat and ineffective. Separating theory and practice leads to practitioners who implement other people's theories without regard for what is possible from the individual and the organization. In our office there are no divisions between thinking and doing. The actual physical environment is not divided in ways that separate people physically. There is a constant exchange of ideas and support for each other's work. We have spontaneous and percolating discussions in the public space we've created in our physically and philosophically open office, which leads to acceptance for thinking, contributing, creativity, and learning.

Working this way requires time. And time is money. Taking time for ideas and process, especially in the current environment, is seen as inefficient. Time is something bureaucracies control. We see this in the increasing application of business models being applied in government. In the long run, operating this way stifles creativity, new ideas, collaborations, citizen engagement, and structures that allow different voices to be heard. Business models or standardization has us doing the same things over and over again, in the same way. The inherent belief is that people must be managed and controlled in order to get results. Inherent also is the belief that there are those among us who are capable and those who must be made to be "effective."

The critiques can be quite harsh when you try to have an organization that functions counter to the current business ethos. There is a real cost to your personal and professional credibility and competency. The critique is you are disorganized, can't meet deadlines, lack follow through, have too much process and dialogue, or that you are not producing or working effectively. However, when you produce high quality work this way you challenge the prevailing structures in the institution.

We believe the degree to which process is denigrated in an organization is an indicator of both how rigidly organized the organization is and the degree to which it is moving toward a nonhierarchical way of working. When a rigid organization is seriously challenged, and begins moving away from that way of operating, then the resistance intensifies. We have witnessed during our tenure in city government a change from being annoyed with process and a humorous tone around it ("Seattle processes things to death.") to contempt for process and an emphasis on form over content. Yet, this contempt may reflect the degree to which the organization is being challenged. And this is a good thing.

Both see their work as a vocation. For Evelyn, vocation means "dedicated to a cause by making change beyond work. Life work." For Sheila, vocation is "how I would lead my life, no matter where I am . . . with an intact value base, making change for myself and for people I care for." They are the change they wish to see in the world.

Their work for the city of Seattle is groundbreaking and germinal. The Domestic and Sexual Violence Prevention Office evolved from a task force of activists formed to look at the question of the role of city government in preventing domestic and sexual violence. Prior to this time, domestic and sexual violence was seen exclusively as a criminal/police matter. The task force made a number of recommendations to the mayor, one of which was the formation of concerted institutional and policy efforts to prevent domestic and sexual violence, citywide. Two bodies were formed: a policy-making body—the Domestic Violence Council—and the Domestic and Sexual Violence Prevention Office. The office is responsible for drafting and directing the city's response to domestic violence. The office is a relatively independent unit, with great autonomy to define and direct policy and implementation. Its work is grounded in primarily a feminist analysis of violence against women—primarily a critique of patriarchy and white supremacy.

One of the things that makes the office unique is the problem it addresses: violence against women. There are very few policy and planning offices in government centered on this issue. Evelyn and Sheila agree that it is difficult to maintain an activist role within government.

Once you engage in that process, you are now a part of it and it's off and running. The difficulty is not just that you are up against the system; the difficulty is the tensions between activists in government and activists outside of government. If you are in government, the support and dialogue and ideas around activism are minimal. If they exist at all they are not part of the structure you are in. At the same time there is an erosion of support for your work outside government that contributes to feeling isolated. Since the work is hard, not having the support is difficult. It is understandable: you make better salaries, you have access to power, and you are part of that power structure. On the other hand, this work is in many ways more difficult for exactly those same reasons. The forces within government organizations working against new ideas make it difficult to act as social change agents. We have to get better at connecting the activism in the community with the activism in government.

Social change is not what government does, it is claimed, but as Evelyn says "My God, why not and who better to do it?" They both choose to practice their advocacy within government, instead of outside of government. Sheila says:

I work in government because it is a place and a vehicle for a great deal to happen. There is a great potential for fundamental, structural change in our society. You have the ability to create change and to help those who are outside of government. I feel we both bring our collective and historical experience to city government on issues of men's violence against women and to communities on working and influencing city government on violence against women. I feel it is a good place to do this work, to foster access and engagement and to do so, fortunately, in an office that is a learning environment. Of course, we are talking about a specific government, a specific office, a specific leadership in this office that allows me to feel this way. I believe reclaiming our government is serious activism.

Evelyn speaks to the paucity of activists within government:

As far as bringing a value base that challenges existing structures and assumptions those structures are based on, there's not a whole lot of this. A part of me wants to do this work. The reality here is that government is having a tremendous impact on women and children on a daily basis and to not have anyone within government critiquing government's roles and changing some of the underlying relationships is problematic. It is not that there are bad people in government, but that it will roll on the way it is rolling. To me it is both a conscious choice and a responsibility to be here in government.

They have words of advice for other activists within government: understand your organization and know organizational theory because "it will point out places where you can do your activism and build allies. Having allies is essential in maintaining a radical voice. Sticking and remaining true to your values is really important because you can be asked to sacrifice a great deal." They say that one must know who one is and the extent of one's obligations or responsibilities to others. There are times one has to protect one's job, "as women with children, we all know this. . . . I think you do have to make choices sometimes to back down or find another way. Strategic thinking is really important."

In addition, we need to pay very close attention to the kinds of spaces that are cultivated in the work environment. "Pay attention to your home, your office, your group. How we treat each other, how you support one another. . . . Hierarchical systems are destructive." Central are relationships. Sheila says:

We have elevated relationships to the top priority of what we do. The policies and procedures are necessary and you have to understand them, but the relationships are the fundamental difference in how we work. Now, everybody

In Their Words

Evelyn Brom

*What lessons would you like to share with others who want
to practice transformational public service?*

To practice transformational public service it is important to develop a supportive network of allies and to involve communities, which is strategic and democratic and in itself transformational. Transformational public service builds community by using emotional intelligence and good listening skills. In building trust, public servants encourage dialogue and meaningful problem solving.

An example of a project illustrating transformational public service is our Multilingual Access Project (MAP). MAP brings together community-based agency representatives in a planning process that will assert access to social and legal institutions as a basic human right and will make funding recommendations to city policy makers. This project team is entirely women of color, with a community-organizing consultant facilitating the monthly meetings. MAP recognizes the many ways we provide leadership in our communities. The city pays participating agencies for their staff's involvement and sharing of expertise.

has relationships. What is different here, I think, is in the way we do our work and also in what we say. Relationships are paramount. We focus on building genuine relationships where respect and honor are at the center; we are not, necessarily, focused on relationships as alliances, as relationships are usually defined in government. Genuine relationships are based upon respect, inclusiveness, value-centered interactions, learning what is important to people in their work and where you come together with that person, and sharing strengths. When we build genuine relationships, we begin to change the culture of an organization. The organizational culture is where the transformation has to take place—it is the culture that is really the engine that really makes things work. All the other things that are out there—policy, procedures, discussions, talking with city council, the analysis of a particular bill—are pretty routine and you can bring your own political analysis to that. The real change is how we treat each other as we do this work. How we bring people into the process, who has a voice, and where the respect comes from. That, to me, is at core about how you begin to shift these organizations—that has to become key, and it is not yet.

Finally, one has to take care of oneself. For both Sheila and Evelyn the ability to talk about and deconstruct ideas and processes at work is animating and sustaining. Their support for each other is crucial. As one said, "We trust each other's motivations and we trust each other's value base—once you have that, there is room for disagreement or conflict. It is safe to be upset with each other without it being devastating." Being surrounded by like-minded colleagues is a gift. They also, however, have to engage in activities outside of work that animate and sustain them, which includes creative outlets, reading fiction, and family.

Note

Evelyn and Sheila have since resigned from the City of Seattle and joined the consulting group Blakely House Design, Media and Communications, a firm in the Seattle area. While they worked effectively in citiy government for many years, a change in administration during the writing of this book prompted their decision to leave. They believed their skills and expertise would be of better use outside government at the current time. However, they continue to feel strongly that activism inside government is not only possible but also critical. They refer you to Joe Gray's story for a sense of how their story has changed since this was written.

In collaboration with communities, they continue their work to improve government and community responses to violence against women and provide technical assistance to those public and nonprofit administrators receiving Violence Against Women Act (VAWA) federal grants.

Comment

Theory and Practice

The man who never alters his opinion is like standing water,
and breeds reptiles of the mind.

—William Blake

As Evelyn and Shelia's story illuminates, practice cannot be separated from theory in transformational public administration. In this book we undertake, in part, to articulate an argument for applying a particular kind of theory to public administration. In doing so, we draw on several theoretical traditions: classical critical theory (the Frankfurt school), liberation theory (Antonio Gramsci and Paulo Freire), American pragmatism (John Dewey, William James, and Cornell West) and depth psychology (Carl Jung and his contemporary followers). We seek to weave these four traditions together into a contemporary form of critical theory that is deeply germane to public service.

Why pursue a contemporary critical theory of public administration? Public administration, after all, is the study of the manner in which the will of the state (the public interest) is carried out by the administrative arm. One might understandably ask, where is there room for a theory of public administration and public service that draws into question the will of the state?

We argue that there is, indeed, a great deal of room for critical theory in public administration in that it organizes both thought and action. Critical theory explores unexamined assumptions and compares those with lived experience. The contradictions so often discussed in public administration theory—between efficiency and democracy, between politics and administration, between self-interest and collective benefits, between active and passive forms of citizenship—are cast, in traditional theories, as opposite tendencies that cannot be satisfied simultaneously. Critical theory allows us to see these as something other than irresolvable or intractable contradictions and, as a result, imagine different ways of being.

Critical theory also provides an ethical impulse toward substantive equality and democracy. Related to the ethical impulse are the important psychoanalytic insights critical theory offers. The original critical theorists broke important theoretical ground by incorporating Freudian theory as a means for explaining societal theories of repression. Herbert Marcuse (1941/1960; 1964), in particular, explored the psychodynamics involved in the installation of repression in the individual and collective psyche. He argued that repression is reproduced both *within* the individual and *over* the individual. Thus, repression is in this sense both a psychological and political phenomenon. By integrating depth psychology, a Jungian approach to psychoanalytic theory, we offer both personal and political response to this oppression.

Finally, we argue that critical theory offers an important role for the administrator. Drawing on Antonio Gramsci's conception of the intellectual, we contend that the administrator can be an important "bridge" between the state and civil society, providing access in a manner that contributes to both personal and societal transformation. Indeed, critical theory is the foundation of transformational public service.

Critical theory is not generally addressed in textbooks of public administration (see, however, Denhardt, 1981, and Box, 2004). One probable reason is that critical theory can quickly become mired in obscure and irrelevant-sounding jargon, thus almost automatically suggesting that it is a worldview imbued with impractical and unsuitable applications for everyday public service. Additionally, many scholars in the field of critical theory reinforce this perception of impracticality, in that they frequently represent themselves as "theorists" and not "practitioners."

We cannot help but note the ironies here. As originally constructed, critical theory was deliberately intended to unite theory with practice by helping restore self-reflection and understanding to individuals who had become flattened and deadened under the influence of instrumental reason. The original goal of critical theory was practical—to help reveal the socially constructed nature of the world, to explain that ossified social constructs passing as reality are changeable, and then to work to transform society as the expression of an emancipatory vision.

If one breaks free of the jargon, critical theory essentially represents a practice of guiding principles, in the same sense that one might practice mindfulness or nonviolence from a Buddhist or Yogic perspective. The emphasis, here, is on practice—both the things we do and the things we constantly work at doing. A practice is never finalized; it is always in process, constantly being examined and adjusted. A practice is an ever-renewing process, something we live every day. In this way, practices require that we be both reflective and self-critical. Practices also require that we "do our own work," theoretically, ideologically, and psychologically. We note that those who work in the fields of public administration are called *practitioners* and that they *practice* public service. We present a vision and interpretation of this practice in the next section.

What Is Critical Theory?

Although we may hear about it a great deal, the term "critical theory" actually has a rather imprecise meaning. Historically, it was often used to refer a group of scholars and their collective school of social theory. At the same time, it encompasses a broader reference to a method of self-conscious critique aimed at change and emancipation (see Giroux, 1983).

The school of thought associated with critical theory is commonly referred to as the Frankfurt school, although its proper title was the Institut für Sozialforschung—the Institute for Social Research—founded in 1923 as an affiliate of the University of Frankfurt. The institute became an academic home to Max Horkheimer, Theodor Adorno, Leo Lowenthal, Walter Benjamin, Franz Neumann, Eric Fromm, and Herbert Marcuse, although they were not all in full-time residence.

It is not our intention here to describe the Frankfurt school's work; much of the historical development of the Frankfurt school is well captured by others (see, among others, Arato & Gebhart, 1982/1994; Giroux, 1983; and Agger, 1991, 1992). It is sufficient here to know that part of the meaning of the term critical theory is a reference to the collective body of work that emerged from the scholars of the Frankfurt school.

The term critical theory, although its spirit and theoretical orientation owe much to Kant, Hegel, and Marx, appears to have been first used by Horkheimer (1937/1976) in an essay in which he attempted to distinguish between traditional theory and what he called critical theory. Horkheimer contended that traditional theory focused on deriving generalizations about the world, whether these generalizations were arrived at deductively (as with Cartesian theory), inductively (as with John Stuart Mill), or phenomenologically (as with Husserlian philosophy). Horkheimer pointed out that the social sciences were different from the natural sciences: generalizations could not easily be made from so-called experiences because the understanding of experience was being fashioned from ideas that were in the observer him or herself. The observer is simultaneously part of what s/he is observing, and caught in a specific historical context in which ideologies unavoidably shape one's thinking. Thus theory would be conforming to the ideas in the mind of the observer rather than the experience itself. (This is also the basis of contemporary theories in the natural sciences, particularly physics—that the observed itself changes in the very act of observation.) In other words, thought, understanding, experience, and even the act of observation are not neutral, self-contained, detached, or objective. They are all unavoidably influenced by social and historical forces.

Horkheimer, in making this argument, injected the idea of reification (making something appear real when it is not), contending that the development of theory "was absolutized, as though it were grounded in the inner nature of knowledge as such or justified in some other ahistorical way, and thus it became a reified, ideological category" (1937/1976, p. 212). This was later to become the basis for another charge that traditional theory maintained a strict (and erroneous) separation between thought and action. In contrast, critical theory was about insight and reflection leading toward praxis and emancipation. It was to be a *social theory* with *practical intent.* In this regard, Horkheimer was echoing Marx: the point of philosophy is to change to work, not just to interpret it.

For Horkheimer, approaches to understanding in the social sciences cannot simply imitate those in the natural sciences (a phenomenon some social scientists have labeled "physics envy"). What is required Horkheimer argues, is "a radical reconsideration not of the scientist alone but of the knowing individual as such" (1937/1976, p. 221). However, the epistemological turn gave critical theory a critique of a different kind. Critical theory was about being *self*-critical. It rejected any pretensions to absolute truth (and thus anticipated postmodernism). As has been noted elsewhere (see Zanetti, 1997), critical theory defends the primacy of neither matter (materialism) nor consciousness (idealism), arguing that both distort reality to the benefit, eventually, of some small group. In other words, neither practice nor ideas can dominate in some envisioned "best of" hierarchy.

While critical theory must at all times be self-critical, Horkheimer insisted a theory is critical only if it is explanatory, practical, and normative all at the same time. As Bohman (1996) states in summarizing Horkheimer's criteria: they "must *explain* what is wrong with current social reality, *identify* actors to change it, and provide clear norms for criticism and practical *goals* for the future" (p. 190; emphasis added). The focus of critical theory, as we said earlier, is not simply to mirror reality, but to change it. In Horkheimer's words, the goal of critical theory is "the emancipation of human beings from the circumstances that enslave them" (1937/1976, p. 219, see also p. 224).

Additionally, the Frankfurt school proposed and utilized a <u>dialectical</u> logic. Adorno (1966/1973), for example, denied the foundation on which all knowledge is presumed to rest. Instead, like others in the Frankfurt school, he put forth the view that there was a constant interplay of particular and universal, of moment and totality. From this dynamic relationship *contradictions* emerge and become apparent. The resolutions of these contradictions eventually promote the generation of a new totality (the three familiar moments of dialectic: thesis, antithesis, and synthesis).

It is this ability to see the negative (the contradiction, the shadow) and use it dynamically that is so essential to the practice of critical theory. In a recently translated work, Marcuse (circa unknown/1993) tried to explain why intellectual oppositions often become ineffective and impotent. A key concept in this explanation was the notion of the "estrangement effect," or what we might today call "shock value." Marcuse argues that the estrangement effect becomes an artistic-political device only to the extent that the estrangement can be maintained "to produce the shock which may bare the true relationship between the two worlds and languages: the one being the positive negation of the other" (p. 187) (Carr & Zanetti, 1999).

This estrangement effect—shock value—is at the heart of dialectical logic and thinking. Dialectical thinking is destructive, but the destruction reemerges as a positive act. Estrangement (shock) produces emotional disturbance, turmoil, and discomfort. It runs counter to prevailing attitudes and modes of thought. Those who benefit from the status quo do not appreciate it, and often attach their own normative value judgments (often calling estrangement phenomena "vulgar," "immoral," "unpatriotic," or "un-American"). But this estrangement is part of a necessary process because it creates the conditions for seeing the world anew, in the form of the synthesis (new possibilities, a new status quo).

Frederic Jameson notes that dialectical thinking deliberately reacts to our habitual practices, ideologies, and views of the world. Thus, when "common sense" predominates and characterizes our normal, everyday environment, "dialectical thinking presents itself as the perversely hairsplitting, as the overelaborate and the oversubtle, reminding us that the simple is in reality only a simplification, and that *the self-evident draws its force from hosts of buried presuppositions*" (Jameson, 1971, p. 308; emphasis added). But we have only to recall the times (1776, in the Declaration of Independence and 1789, in the preamble to the Constitution) when "common sense" told us that blacks and women were not capable of participating responsibly in government to understand that "self-evident truths" are often self-evident only to a privileged few.

Why a Critical Theory of Public Administration and Public Service?

As mentioned earlier, critical theory is not typically discussed in public administration texts. We believe this omission should be remedied, especially if one seeks to practice public service in such a way as to promote significant social change—if one seeks to practice transformational public service. Specifically, we find critical theory meaningful to and for public service for the following four reasons.

1. *Critical theory opens the doors to new possibilities for theory and practice by exploring unexamined assumptions and comparing these with the resonance of lived experience.*

The very logic of critical theory demands that one learn to excavate assumptions and reveal contradictions. By looking at habits, situations, communities, and relationships with new eyes, we often begin to see more clearly the elements that had been overlooked before. In the language of organizational theorist Chris Argyris (1971), we learn to articulate the espoused theory and compare it with the theory in use. Are we doing what we say? Do we say what we mean? Are our theories and structures of democratic equality serving us in the manner we need? If not, how are our practices reifying (making real) things that do not serve?

These questions are being asked publicly with greater and greater frequency. For example, the November 2003 National Public Radio (NPR) series "Whose Democracy Is It?" noted blatant contradictions in American democracy such as the disparate numbers of millionaires in Congress, the logistical difficulties that impede universal suffrage, and the integrity of the current voting system. Many of the same problems have been noted by Paul Krugman (2002). These works showed how critical theory plays out in our world; critical theory plays an important role in articulating alternative interpretations of both current and historical social phenomena (see the connections with liberation theory below).

2. *The contradictions so often discussed in public administration theory—between efficiency and democracy, between politics and administration, between self-interest and collective benefits, between active and passive forms of citizenship—are cast as opposite tendencies that cannot be satisfied simultaneously. Critical theory allows us to cast these in a dialectical relationship, with the intention that instead of claiming "truth" in one or the other, we, instead, let the contradiction stand.*

We, as scholars, practitioners, and citizens, have been reared with, and trained in, the Western principle of noncontradiction. In our math and logic and research classes, we learn that something cannot be *a* and *not-a* simultaneously. Traditional (or formal) logic dictates that two contradictory elements can never be true together (see, for example, Karl Popper's philosophy of science, 1963). But traditional logic, because it focuses on empirical (mostly quantitative) representations of reality, necessarily builds on arbitrarily constructed foundations—that is, we have to start somewhere, so why not here? At some point, however, the logic necessarily becomes abstracted from reality, despite recent efforts to render the decision process more subtle, as in fuzzy logic. Again, one has only to recall the simplified graphs of supply and demand one learns in elementary economics to understand what we mean by this kind of abstraction. Those graphs assume that we are all rational and self-interested, but we all know they ignore many anomalies—for example, those who purchase organic or recycled goods, even though they are more expensive, or those who refuse to purchase certain sports or clothing labels because their labor practices are said to be abusive and inhumane.

In critical theory, however, form is not separated from content. Logic must continually reflect the whole of reality, not just an abstraction of it. Critical theory allows us to break out of the prevailing dichotomous, black-and-white logic and advocates a search for synthesis rather than compromise or even consensus, since both compromise and consensus contain elements of potential domination and intimidation.

3. *Critical theory provides an ethical impulse toward substantive equality and democracy.*

The epistemological basis of critical theory requires a very specific approach, one that is both teleological (about the ends) and deontological (about ethics). In describing the critical perspective, Egon Guba and Yvonna S. Lincoln (1994) note that critical theory is informed by historical realism, an approach that views reality as shaped by social, political, cultural, economic, ethnic, and gender considerations that have ossified over time and are now, mistakenly, assumed to be fixed, a priori conditions. These reified structures have become a kind of virtual reality—as in, "that's just the way things are." As Guba and Lincoln state:

> Thus, a critical perspective seeks restitution for historical wrongs and emancipation for individuals that are trapped by these hardened societal structures. There is a moral tilt toward revelation and the erosion of ignorance, incorporating values of empowerment and altruism and combining them with a stimulus to action. The critical perspective requires a *transformative intellectual* to act as advocate and activist, and, interestingly, demands a kind of re-socialization—including the understanding and mastery of quantitative analytical techniques that can be utilized for both traditional and *transformative purposes.* (1994, p. 110; emphasis added)

4. *Related to the ethical impulse are the important psychoanalytic insights critical theory offers.*

The original critical theorists broke important theoretical ground by incorporating Freudian theory as a means for explaining societal theories of repression. Among other things, Marcuse was reacting to the work of Freud, particularly Freud's *Totem and Taboo* (1913) and *Civilization and Its Discontents* (1930), in which Freud explores the relationship between civilization and the individual. In *Totem and Taboo* Freud describes his theory of the primal murder of the father by his sons, an episode that he imagines represents the founding act of civilization (the contract among the brothers, in which they mutually agree to renounce their claim to unfettered sexual and aggressive drives in return for the benefits of an ordered social life). This establishment of prohibitions (against incest and against patricide) is, in Freud's view, the essential human condition: the "constituitive act through which a law-governed social world is created, namely, the Oedipally structured social <u>ontology</u> of civilization" (Whitebook, 1995, p. 22).

Horkheimer and Adorno, in *Dialectic of Enlightenment* (1944/1972), critiqued Freud's analysis by arguing that in order to conquer the external world (create civilization), humans first had to conquer their inner worlds—that is, they had to transform themselves into disciplined, purposive agents of a bureaucratized and administered society. Horkheimer and Adorno's basic thesis was that the domination of the inner world ultimately made emancipation impossible. They tried to imagine a utopian transfiguration of civilization but, ultimately, could not envision any alternative in which the regressive features were not more disturbing than the prospect itself. It is this theoretical cul-de-sac that has challenged critical theorists ever since: how to put the theory into practice (Whitebook, 1995; Zanetti, 1997). Nonetheless, this conundrum (one must overcome the domination of the inner world in order to overcome domination in the external world) is an essential element of transformational public service: in order to transform the world, we begin with ourselves and move out, in small circles, from there.

Critical theory can get us to many of the places we would like to go, yet, in our experience, we also need to draw on other theoretical forms to make a contemporary critical theory that is shaped for public service. These include liberation theory (which owes much to Gramsci's work), pragmatism, and psychoanalytical theory/depth psychology.

Liberation Theory

We use the term "liberation theory" to encompass a general orientation toward learning and change, especially in adults. Most often, this orientation takes the late Paulo Freire, Brazilian activist and educator, as its intellectual focus. Freire is widely considered to have been one of the most important influences in education during the twentieth century (Mayo, 1999). Although born into a middle-class family, Freire experienced extreme deprivation and hunger as a result of the global impact of the Great Depression. He later stated that this experience allowed him to connect with the lives of the desperately poor.

Freire, who was educated as a lawyer and later earned a Ph.D., became active in adult literacy as part of the Popular Culture movement. His book, *Pedagogy of the Oppressed* (1970/2000), is both an educational and political effort because though achieving literacy, the poor became eligible to vote. His success in this arena, however, brought him to the attention of political reactionaries, who arrested him and later forced him into exile. When he returned to his native country sixteen years later, Freire became active in the Workers Party and consulted on literacy campaigns in Grenada and Nicaragua, eventually becoming the national education secretary of Brazil. He also continued to work closely with scholars and activists he had met during his exile, including Myles Horton, founder of the Highlander Folk School in Tennessee.

Philosophically, liberation theory relies heavily on the work of Antonio Gramsci, an Italian philosopher and political activist who spent much of his adult life imprisoned for his activism. Liberation theory also relies upon the liberation theology movement of the 1970s. Liberation theory currently has threads of scholarship and activism in a number of different disciplines. Some well-known exponents of liberation theory include bell hooks (feminism, pedagogy), Augusto Boal (theatre), and Henry Giroux and Peter McLaren (education). For all of these individuals, understanding the social world involves recognizing the extent to which our lives are constructed, affected, and punctuated by official narratives (which are also sometimes referred to as dominant discourses, hegemony, or grand narratives). Liberation occurs when individuals learn to identify these narratives, compare them with their lived experiences, and begin to construct counternarratives that highlight how certain groups have been marginalized, silenced, subjugated, or forgotten in the dominant discourse.

One of Gramsci's most important theoretical contributions was his articulation of hegemony. According to Gramsci (as stated by Fontana, 1993, p. 140), hegemony is the

> intellectual and moral leadership (*direzione*) whose principal constituting elements are consent and persuasion. A social group or class can be said to assume a hegemonic role to the extent that it articulates and proliferates throughout society cultural and ideological belief systems whose teachings are accepted as universally valid by the general population. Ideology,

culture, philosophy, and their "organizers"—the intellectuals—are thus intrinsic to the notion of hegemony. Hegemony necessarily implies the creation of a particular structure of knowledge and a particular system of values. The social group or class that is capable of forming its own particular knowledge and value systems, and of transforming them into general and universally applicable conceptions of the world, is the group that exercises intellectual and moral leadership.

Hegemony is presented as an equilibrium between civil society and political society, where civil society represents institutions such as the church, the family, and the schools, and political society is represented by the state (the formal political institutions and officials). In Gramsci's conception, power is both centralized in the political system and diffused across civil institutions. Consent is organized, and power exercised, not just through official political policies and practices, but also in civil society, where many aspects of social and political identity are fundamentally grounded (Carroll & Ratner, 1994). The dynamics of force and consent, power and persuasion are intertwined. Power cannot be maintained for very long by force alone. In order to continue to exert influence, a dominant group must also gain the consent of the subordinate group by convincing subordinates that their best interests are served by accepting the prevailing order.

Given the interaction between force (power) and consent (persuasion), Gramsci argued that repressive institutions must be challenged within the context of transforming popular consciousness both as a precondition for transformation and as a central aspect of the liberation itself (Holub, 1992). As oppressed individuals and communities become aware of the (artificial) limitations placed on them by society, they may expand their perceptions of their needs and demands. With this understanding, they can take the initiative to move beyond the boundaries that previously contained them (keeping them "in their place," so to speak).

For the purposes of our work, the important aspects of liberation theory include the following points:

1. *Change requires not only rational-cognitive activity, but a passionate, emotional commitment and an intense partisanship rooted in everyday political struggle.*

In liberation theory, change emerges as part of an organic process, of which the transformation of consciousness is a necessary component (Boggs, 1976). This is sometimes referred to as an evolution toward counterhegemony. Along with the existence of power is the possibility for resistance. To struggle against power, subjects must create a new constellation of rights. Social-political movements are the generators of these new political forms (Foucault, 1984).

What motivates marginalized social groups to challenge the hegemonic structure? Conversely, what contributes to quiescence? The process of change is both internal and external, as we explain below.

2. *Gramsci's praxis is a dialectical interaction between the degree to which human activity is shaped (determined) by external structures, and the ability of human activity to transform those structures. Liberation theory, like critical theory, provides a framework for understanding the social and political processes of power and powerlessness.*

The specific context we wish to address here is what Steven Lukes (1974) and John Gaventa (1980) have termed the "third dimension" of political power relationships. The first two dimensions refer to what political scientists often call pluralist and elitist theories. Very simply, pluralist theories of political group interaction assume a fairly open political system and equal access for all interested parties. In Robert A. Dahl's well-known definition, "A has power [or influence] over B to the extent that [A] can get B to do something that B would not otherwise do" (1956, pp. 202–3). In this conception of political activity, inaction is the result of apathy, inertia, or choice. Because all individuals have access to the political system, nonparticipation reflects little more than personal preference.

Elitist theories recognize that bias exists in the political system, or, in the words of Elmer Schattschneider (1960, p. 105), "the heavenly chorus sings with a distinct upper class accent." Because not all political players have equal access to resources, the result is that some groups, players, or issues become "organized out" of the system (ibid., p. 105). Important to our discussion, however, is the assumption within this framework that an absence of grievance equals some form of political consensus or agreement. A power struggle can be seen to exist when both sides are aware of it, or even when the less powerful party is aware of it (because the powerful are so entrenched as to be oblivious to challenge).

In the "third dimension" of political power, however, Gramsci's dynamics of hegemony are acknowledged. Lukes (1974, p. 34) argues that in this conception, "A exercises power over B when A affects B in a manner contrary to B's interests." More importantly, "A may exercise power over B by getting him to do what he does not want to do, but he *also exercises power over him by influencing, shaping, or determining his very wants*" (p. 23; emphasis added). In other words, A affects B by shaping B's very conceptions of the issues altogether. This consideration of political power takes into account the many ways in which potential issues are kept out of the political arena through the operation and influence of social forces and institutional practices (Gaventa, 1980).

Understanding this third dimension of political power gives an explanation for how power shapes the participation patterns of the marginalized or relatively powerless. The power processes are located in the social construction of meanings and patterns that encourage B to act in a manner that is to A's benefit and B's detriment. The relative power and powerlessness of A and B are reinforced over time and maintained not by the fear of A's power, but by B's conviction of her own powerlessness, often manifested as fatalism, self-deprecation, or apathy. This sense of powerlessness leads to internalization of the values, beliefs, and rules of the powerful as a kind of adaptive response. The powerless become socialized into compliance (Gaventa, 1980). This is the essence of Gramsci's conception of hegemony.

Simple domination is not sufficient for retaining power, at least not for long. A social group or class whose power is derived solely from coercion cannot achieve lasting rule. Only when this social group constructs a sociopolitical order capable of instilling its moral and cultural beliefs in the consciousness of the people can it achieve a more stable hegemony.

As oppressed individuals become aware of the limitations placed on them by society, they expand their perceptions of their needs and demands. They can take the initiative to move beyond the boundaries that have contained them. The dominant group must exercise intellectual and moral leadership to impress upon the people a particular conception of the world. But this dynamic also means that change can only be achieved dialectically—if simple domination does not work, neither does simple protest or even "simple" revolution. Hegemony can only be toppled when the marginalized consciously enter the hegemonic frame and use its own rules and methods to construct a counterhegemony, while at the same time resisting co-optation (Fontana, 1993), or to paraphrase of Audre Lorde's words, mentioned earlier, using the master's tools to tear down the master's house.

A particularly compelling version of this struggle is recounted in John Gaventa's *Power and Powerlessness: Quiescence and Rebellion in an Appalachian Valley* (1980). In this book, Gaventa recounts the manner in which the citizens of the Clear Fork Valley learned, over decades, to challenge the economic and political power of the American Association, Ltd., a British corporation formed for the purposes of mining coal and iron from the region. As in many colonization processes, the residents were persuaded to sell their land for nearly nothing—and eventually, the unequal distribution of land and resources came to be viewed as an unchangeable element of the social structure. Descendants of the original settlers came to view their forefathers' actions as the result of "ignorance" and internalized the sense of shame and responsibility. This internalized powerlessness is what creates quiescence—a socialized compliance and reluctance to question the "official" way of things.

We might also take Gramsci's own life as an illustration of this process. Marginalized in one way or another all his life, Gramsci drew inspiration from his experiences to illuminate and bring life to his theoretical constructs. Gramsci perceived his life experiences dialectically, locating his political and cultural marginalization within a greater context and sought to bring about synthesis (transformation) through direct participation in the problems posed by history.

Gramsci was born in Sardinia at an important juncture in that island's history. At that point, the island had been a part of the Kingdom of Italy for thirty years, but it was a site of much greater poverty than the rest of the kingdom. The system of *latifundia* (great manorial estates descended from Roman times) remained in place and most of the island's inhabitants lived in miserable socioeconomic conditions. The Kingdom of Italy brought innovations to the island in the form of concessions of the coal mines to foreign financiers and increasing agricultural commerce with France. The former contributed to the establishment of exploitative working conditions for the miners, who were economically captive to the concession holders; the latter threw the island into economic crisis when the French market was closed to Sardinian exports in 1887. The conflation of these conditions and events sharpened the internal contradictions of the island (tremendous wealth contrasted with dire poverty), and also revealed Sardinia's extreme backwardness in comparison to the rest of the kingdom.

Francesco Gramsci, Antonio's father, became caught up in the local political struggle and was sentenced to jail, throwing the family into destitution. While his father was actively involved in local politics, Gramsci, however, did not become involved in politics until he moved to Turin to attend the university. There he was greatly influenced by the antipositivist polemic of the time and became sympathetic to a Hegelian-dialectical reading of Marxism. Eventually, he abandoned his studies for political activism. It was in this cultural context that he came to understand his experiences as a Sardinian, revealed in his increasingly political interpretation of Marx's writings. He became involved in practical politics in the Turinese factory councils, struggling for workers' rights and participatory democracy in governing the factories.

Though Gramsci was certainly influenced by the political marginalization of Sardinia within the Kingdom of Italy, he was also influenced by his marginalized status in the personal sphere, as well. Sickly and physically malformed, he suffered lifelong prejudices arising from his bodily differences. Additionally, through his university studies of linguistics, he became aware of the powerful influence of language in the establishment and maintenance of cultural hegemony. His mother's familiarity with Sardinian folklore was a source of inspiration in understanding the cultural knowledge and identity that such local stories carry. This understanding contributed to Gramsci's awareness of the literary, cultural, and educational dynamics in which hegemony is instilled and maintained by privileging certain "purified" forms of intellectualism over more popular manifestations of knowledge.

Perhaps the most important aspect Gramsci's "philosophy of praxis" was that praxis (theoretically informed practical action) must be contextual. Political change cannot be preprogrammed or conceived apart from current conditions; theoretical discussion must remain open to new contributions arising from practice, and constantly verified in relation to historical conditions and popular experience. (Gramsci was adamantly opposed to the American philosophy of pragmatism precisely because it omitted the historical context of experience.) The point of departure must always be culture as a whole, not a set of doctrines torn from their original context.

The important point we wish to make here is that our social embeddedness is more complex than early theories of revolution might have suggested. For example, students of psychology often learn of the "Asch effect"—the phenomenon in which an isolated individual will conform to a group's erroneous version of reality, while the presence of a single ally can help the individual to resist. Here, the context of Solomon Asch's research and life are germane. Asch's experience as a political minority—he was a member of the Communist Party while at Brooklyn College—may have contributed to his important psychological discovery and his research also illustrated how a small group can resist the irrational consensus of a majority.

Cleansing the political context from the history of psychology contributed to the construction of the "abstract individual." The construction of such an individual (the nameless, faceless, masculine subject) enabled psychology to become a useful "administrative science" for the purpose of social control. Political action emphasizes the dynamic character of social actors shaping societies and building social institutions. Furthermore, the conception of political action specifically takes into account the function of overcoming dominant ideology. Ideology, as we use it here, refers to a system of ideas that promotes particular interests, typically by fostering ideas that distort, deny, or conceal historical contexts. Ideology constructs reality in a way that convinces the marginalized to accept and internalize negative attributions of themselves as natural and legitimate. In a self-fulfilling cycle, people then come to behave in accordance with these perceptions (Lukes, 1974; Gaventa, 1980).

(Critical) Pragmatism

The honoring of practice-in-practice is the essence of pragmatism, the third foundation we use for this book. Pragmatism is a distinctly American philosophy that has enjoyed its popularity in waves. It emerged at the end of the nineteenth century, was hugely influential in the early part of the twentieth, but suffered criticism and decline after World War II. Somewhat surprisingly, pragmatism was "rehabilitated" in the 1980s and fused with continental theory.

The problem with attempting to summarize this approach, of course, is that there is no one definitive formulation. In the true spirit of pragmatism, each thinker appears to draw together threads that resonate with, and are woven out of, his or her personal experience. Cornell West (1995, p. 315), who considers himself a "prophetic pragmatist," suggests that pragmatism might best be understood as coalescing around three axes: philosophy, theory, and politics.

As West points out, "all pragmatists are epistemic <u>antifoundationalists</u>, though not all epistemic antifoundationalists are pragmatists" (ibid.). That is, all pragmatists subscribe to some version of the abandonment of grand theory. But not all pragmatists agree on the nature of truth, or on the relative strength of the relativist position they embrace—which, he suggests, is closely related to positions on moral theory. Descriptive relativists, for example, claim that fundamental beliefs of people in different communities (cultures) may be similar, yet cultural variations may produce outcomes that differ and even conflict. Weak relativists say that there are some rational procedures or objective standards against which certain beliefs or judgments may be evaluated, but there are no rational criteria for choosing among sets of standards or procedures. Weak relativism effectively endorses a sifting process through which prospective moral procedures or standards must pass. Strong relativists maintain that there is no objective, universal standard that permits one to justify some claims against others. Strong relativism could lead to extreme nihilism, in which no standards are accepted. It could yield a normative relativism, which acknowledges that moral truths and facts exist, but are always relative to a given person, group, or society. Or, strong relativism could produce a metaethical relativism, which holds the view that rival ethical judgments or beliefs can both be right or equally valid.

In his essay "The Fixation of Belief" (1877), Charles S. Peirce establishes four important points upon which other pragmatists build in varying degrees. He articulates a social vision of the scientific enterprise, establishing the community rather than the individual investigator as the primary agent of the cognitive process. Second, he directs the method of science against the entire panorama of inherited beliefs. Third, he contends that open, honest inquiry is morally superior to unthinking loyalty to an inherited belief. And finally, he argues that true belief is simply a "habit" that can remain stable as a "fixed opinion" (Peirce, 1997, p. 19).

In accordance with his reverence for the scientific approach, Peirce derived the authority of his pragmatism from its method. His goal was to demonstrate a relationship between thought, conduct, and feeling to merge intelligence, goodness, and beauty into a "normative science." To do so, it was necessary to commit the community of inquirers to a common approach, subsuming individual differences in the product of the whole (Peirce, 1955).

William James and John Dewey fall somewhere between the extremes of weak and strong relativism. James considered himself an "epistemological realist," claiming that he took for granted the independent existence of reality, and did not consider this independent existence philosophically interesting or relevant. Truth, however, must correspond to what is known from experience. A proposition must be consistent with an individual's stock of existing beliefs, which have stood the test of experience, and it must also yield satisfaction. Dewey likewise argued that all knowledge should be conceived as hypotheses to be tested in experience. In keeping with the colloquial understanding of the word "pragmatic," these two thinkers were primarily concerned with "sensible" approaches and outcomes.

For these pragmatists, truth is provisional, grounded in history and experience. James presented his pragmatism not as philosophy, but as a way of doing philosophy. "It is a method only," he wrote (James, in Dickstein, 1998, p. 3). James insisted that "truth" is not a noun, but a verb. Truth is process: "Truth happens to an idea. It becomes true, is made true by events. . . . Its validity is the process of its validation" (p. 8). Dewey's pragmatism offers an anti-Cartesian psychology in which the self is distributed over a set of projects and experiential interactions. Knowledge, for Dewey, is the outcome of participation in forming or altering the world. This was most evident in his approach to education.

However, Dewey's pragmatism retaines the impulse to forge unity from differences. Like Peirce, Dewey emphasizes the communal nature of inquiry, proceeding from experience and progressing as a result of mutual criticism. Inquiry arises out of a perceived difficulty or disturbance in experience, but Dewey distinguishes between "knowledge" and experience. Experience is not a matter of "knowing"; experience is had. Most philosophers, in Dewey's view, spend entirely too much time exploring knowledge at the expense of what primarily concerns human life: experience. Additionally, Dewey argues that an instrumental-scientific approach to discovery does not necessarily preclude a moral foundation.

We find ourselves most comfortable with Cornell West's version of pragmatism in which he embraces a "radical historicism" that is grounded in a Marxist impulse. Instead of focusing on the status of principles (objective or subjective, necessary or contingent, universal or particular), the radical historicist examines the role and function that such principles play in a culture, community, or society. A radical historicist approach looks at the emergence, dominance, and decline of particular principles under specific social conditions in the historical process (West, 1991, 1995).

The implications of this approach are important. If one disagrees with a particular consensus or community, the task is not to seek philosophical foundations for one's view, but rather to put forward a realizable alternative—a new possibility for consensus and community, and then make it attractive to others (West, 1991, pp. 3–4). It is this process that West calls a *fecund criticism*—that is, a critique in which the primary aim is to discern possibilities in the existing order. This kind of criticism sets two tasks for itself. The first is to avoid the extremes of merely condemning the existing order or endorsing an ideal state of affairs. Instead, a fecund criticism tries to describe, explain, and analyze the present conditions in order to envision an alternative that might be realized. Second, this form of criticism does not simply put forward judgments, or descriptions, or explanations of the present. Its integrity comes from participation in actual political movements that can help create—give birth to—alternatives rooted in the present.

This kind of fecund criticism gives philosophy a more aggressive relationship with the world. As noted earlier, Marx's challenge was that the point of philosophy (theory) was to change the world. It is an acknowledgment that philosophy has a responsibility—an obligation, even—to get its hands dirty in the real world of politics and power, much in the way that Gramsci's "organic intellectual" springs from the mud and dirt of the everyday world (Gramsci, 1971). As West (1991, p. 36) writes, "Any conception of philosophy which ignores this world makes a fetish of criticism and ultimately a fetish of philosophy."

Depth Psychology

Finally, we round out our theoretical framework with the insights of depth psychology—in particular, the work of Carl Jung and his contemporary followers. Jung contended that life is enacted on three levels simultaneously: consciousness, the personal unconscious, and the archetypal or collective unconscious. The ego, our center of consciousness, is like a thin wafer floating on an immense ocean. Beneath that fragile consciousness swirls the personal unconscious, which is also the realm of personal complexes. Complexes are emotionally charged experiences whose intensity derives from the intensity of the original encounter (Hollis, 1994).

In depth psychology, *archetypes* are the contents of the collective unconscious: innate, inherited patterns of psychological performance linked to instinct. Jung viewed archetypes as potential psychic energy inherent in all the typical human life experiences—energy activated uniquely in response to each individual life. An archetype is not a fixed image or fully developed picture (like a photograph), but rather a kind of shadowy primordial form, the content of which is filled by an individual's personal life experiences. According to Jung, archetypes are universal—humans in various cultures possess the same basic archetypal images—although our individual responses to them are entirely unique. We unconsciously internalize the power of these archetypal figures. In the absence of individuation, these patterns and images remain intact at an infantile level (Woodman, 1992, p. 18). When archetypes are activated, they manifest themselves in behaviors and emotions (Samuels, 1997).

For this reason, Jung argued, the primary task of life is to learn to recognize, and come to terms with, those aspects of ourselves that contaminate our perceptions of others. Recognizing our weak or dark traits (those we often try to project onto others) helps us develop a fuller understanding of our interpersonal relations. This cyclical process, called <u>synchronic</u> *individuation,* requires us continually to mediate between our conscious and unconscious, appreciating the paradox and, especially, appreciating the discomfort it produces. Most people are not ready to begin individuation until sometime in midlife. Until then, we are usually too enmeshed in our parental complexes, our psyches are too influenced by the dominant culture around us and we are doing the work of our "first-adulthoods" (Hollis, 1993; Young-Eisendrath, 1995).

As we noted earlier, the first generation Frankfurt school theorists drew on Freudian psychoanalytic theory to explain sociopolitical phenomena. We find Jung's work, in contrast to Freud's, more appropriate to the spirit of critical theory. For example, both approaches recognize and acknowledge the artificial construction of dichotomies. Consequently, both approaches attempt to identify contradictions and resolve them from within, organically and dialectically. Depth psychology provides an additional benefit in that it shows how one can learn to appreciate paradox and live constructively with the discomfort and dissonance it produces. We are not the first to apply depth psychology to the field of public administration (see, for example, Murray, 1997) nor, we hope, will we be the last. There is much to be learned about the practice of public service through the lens of depth psychology and its precursors, the <u>metaphysics</u> of eastern (versus western) thought.

Critical Theory in Action

Gary De La Rosa, Project Coordinator
Human Relations Commission
City of Los Angeles, California

Gary De La Rosa is a fifth generation Californian and an Angeleno. As he used to tell his students: "Half my family conquered the other half of my family. . . . That's why we are so messed up!" He identifies politically as Latino, culturally as Chicano. On his mother's side he is Spanish, Mexican, French, and American Indian. On his father's side he is Mexican and Native American (believed to be Tipi, a small tribe from the San Diego area).

Gary works with the city of Los Angeles Human Relations Commission. He says he does this work because he is a "product of the shadow of history past, known and unknown, which has shaped me and how I look at what I want to do with my life. There have been a series of events that have occurred in the collective past that I had nothing to do with, yet they have helped shape me personally. In a lot of ways, I am a child of the 60s."

Gary grew up in a time of political activism and within an activist family. His father was an active union member (Operating Engineers, Local 12). He remembers accompanying his mother, who was an active member of his school's Parent Teacher Association (PTA), collecting for the local March of Dimes. She also worked the polling booths in the local precinct for elections, eventually becoming a precinct captain. He remembers his house being used as a polling place and people voting in their living room as he and his father sat in the bedroom watching the election results come in. Political activism was a long-standing tradition on his mother's side of the family; one cherished family story is of his mother's grandfather, Encarnacion Bravo, whom she had never seen drunk before, coming home intoxicated for the first time the night that Al Smith lost the presidential election of 1928. "Apparently," Gary says, "he was very disappointed. I guess Al Smith sort of represented the outsider to him, or at least the great Democratic hopeful."

From both sides of the family, Gary received lessons about community. They had an arbor outside of their house and in the summertime, when it was hot, they would sit out under the arbor and tell stories.

I heard stories about my father and his family and learned that he had truly gone through some tough times. Both my parents grew up during the Depression, but my dad's side of the family had it the worst. He was born in the hills east of San Diego. I listened to them talk about how hard it was for poor people then, how people would come into San Fernando, where my mother grew up, looking for work and how my great grandmother would try to help them out by feeding some. From our talks under the arbor, I learned history that was not taught in our school's history class. For example, it was from my mother's experience growing up in San Fernando that I learned of the Japanese American concentration camps in World War II.

During the Depression there was an attempt to move all non-Californian and non-U.S. citizens out of the state in order to get rid of people who were "taking" jobs away from Californians. As I came to learn later, poor Euro-Americans (Dust-Bowl migrants) were being sent back East and people who looked like Mexicans were being kicked across the border. That's what happened to my dad, a United States–born citizen, and his family. As he once told me, he came home from school one day and the next thing he knew he was in Mexico, essentially a foreign country and culture to him. His own country thought he was part of the problem during the Depression and willingly kicked him out. Yet, when they needed cannon fodder for the war effort, they not only brought him back, but drafted him into the Marine Corps!

My father had been an operating engineer before being drafted, and had made good money. However, upon his discharge after World War II he found it hard to find work in his field. He ended up picking fruit, going up and down the California coast and valleys working the produce seasons, following the cycles for almost two years. [Later] when Cesar Chavez got the United Farm Workers Union into the public eye and there were debates going on in the 1960s about whether to support the workers or not, my father would talk to us about those days, about how hard it was to do that work and what that life was like. Many a night under the arbor he'd tell me about those experiences, about the things he'd seen and what he had to do to find work. I gained some understanding and insight about the farm workers laboring through hearing my father's firsthand experience. He'd experienced some of that life and he always had a sense of empathy for their struggle. I think that he passed that sense of empathy for others on to my siblings and me, as did my mother and her family with their accounts of life as they had experienced it. I found it funny later when my father would tease me about my always wanting to help everybody, like giving change to a homeless person for example, advising me to take care of my own. Yet he could be just as guilty as anybody of giving change out to a person in need, or trying to help out his family, for example, over his own needs. Both of my parents were.

My dad's form of activism was through the union and voting. I remember seeing him many times sticking up for the underdog, or what I call the outsiders.

I use that term rather than minorities, for example, to be more inclusive since, depending on where you are at, outsiders includes women, different Euro-American ethnic groups, sexual orientation, and so on. And actually, our closest family friends are from the East Coast and are an example of how I use outsiders. They are Portuguese American and French American, and came out West after World War II. From them I heard stories about what it was like to be a Euro-American ethnic minority on the East Coast and how their communities were often viewed and treated as different and nonmainstream.

I listened to my father talk about the union members needs and occasionally attended union meetings with him where I would hear the debates and the arguments for the union's positions. I'd also hear other workers talk about their experiences growing up during the Depression and World War II. So many of these men had a commonality they could share, and that experience was passed on to me vicariously through listening to them talk about their past and present experiences. It sparked my interest in history and I began to follow the news.

On the other side, my mom was very active in many community events in the late 1950s and 1960s—doing those things that were a part of being a good citizen. This was a by-product I think of both the era she grew up in and of her grandfather's Americanism. She always encouraged my brothers and me to be good citizens, and she really encouraged my interest in politics as well. Meanwhile, I was also beginning to see the acid effects of prejudice and classism and how racism was being played out not only on the national scene on my television, but also locally in my own hometown and neighborhood. I watched and heard of my parents and others in the community experiencing negative things just because of their heritage or their class. All of these experiences and incidents, whether learned collectively or firsthand, these became etched into my memory.

As I've said, my brothers and I were taught that you were supposed to give something back to your community, back to your country. To my mother, it was your patriotic duty. Remember she had been raised by a grandfather who I was often told was very much a patriot, and two of her uncle's had fought in World War I, with one returning. That sense of duty and community came to me not only from my parents, however. First there was the Kennedy era and the "ask not" vibe that challenged people to take part in making this country the best it could be. Youth were being asked to take an active role in moving us forward. I can also remember, a couple of months short of being 10, when Dr. King led the poor people's march on D.C. I remember the speech, or rather remember watching it on the television in August of 1963. It affected me strongly, seeing a sea of people taking action, even if I didn't fully understand all of the issues and nuances of the movement or the moment.

I remember seeing some of the civil rights marches in the South on television, watching marchers leaving or entering Selma and Montgomery, marching over bridges as they entered town. I understood enough of the movement to understand people were not being treated equally, and I knew enough about racism already to feel connected to them in some way. In the summer of 1965 we drove back East to see my uncle who was stationed in North Carolina at the time, and we actually drove by and over some of those very same bridges I'd seen on television. That was living history to me. I also saw some very poor areas and examples of segregation along the way, little towns where at night you'd see African Americans as you entered and left, but never in town center. Those memories stuck. I was beginning to connect in many ways to what was going on countrywide. I began to see the civil rights and the poor people's movement in a much broader context. I began to see it as not just for African Americans or Southerners alone, but for the many other people across the country who were outside the "box." I began to see it as being for me and for people that I knew and lived with . . . . I think, in hindsight, that the civil rights movement has come to be viewed as mostly an African American experience. But I think and remember a broader perspective of who was a part of this movement then, and it began to open my eyes. There were many people on the same side of the fence, poor Euro-Americans, women, American Indians, Niseis. I began to see civil rights as an issue for us as well, meaning those of us here in LA feeling on the outside looking in.

I grew up in Monterey Park, a small town about seven miles east of downtown LA, in the San Gabriel Valley. Monterey Park itself was a fairly diverse place then, in terms of a mix of different Euro-American groups, Nisei or Japanese Americans, and Italian Americans. There was a pretty large Jewish community, some of who were from the Boyle Heights area that had once been a hotbed of Jewish activity and politics in what is sometimes called East Los Angeles today. Monterey Park was a mix of working and middle-class families, of World War II vets trying to obtain the "American dream," of people trying to mix into that great U.S. melting pot.

I had a fairly mixed group of friends growing up, and I learned about diversity in our everyday dealings, though we didn't really know it as that then. We just kind of grew up in that eclectic environment and never really thought of it as anything other than the way it was. Then again the melting pot paradigm was being taught in the schools and through other vehicles of socialization and perhaps that had a part in it. Eventually, I started looking around and noticing that other people weren't necessarily the same way as me in terms of acceptance, and I began to notice some of the prejudices that were being directed towards my friends and me. I also began to notice that adults were treating some of us differently, treating some groups more equal than others, and that soon kids our age, even some of my friends, were mimicking the adults in those attitudes.

I started to figure that there was a connection here in the Los Angeles area between African Americans and Chicanos, poor whites and other outsiders, and that we needed to be a part of the changes that were occurring across the rest of the country. By this time I was in high school and I began to avidly watch the news about the civil rights movement and read more about it. I began to think of the civil rights movement as the first step towards a better United States for those of us non-WASP Euro-Americans, and that it could naturally lead to other outsiders being heard and becoming a part of the progression of change, with each different outsider group getting an opportunity to pull themselves up. I was beginning to connect the outsiders of the U.S. to the history lessons we'd been taught about people in this country being able to succeed if "only they try."

Around the same time I was developing my awareness I learned a new word—assassination. From Medgar Evers and Jack Kennedy to Dr. King and Bobby Kennedy, I began to see a violent side to the fight for the rights I thought, and had been taught, were ours to begin with. In our front room and in our kitchen, we began to see war and injustice live and nightly in vivid black and white. The violence of war and the anger of poverty that we saw on the television began to affect my family and me. By this time both my older brothers were in the Marine Corps and were soon to serve a tour of duty in Viet Nam. This was a time that would both split and unite us. I remember watching the 1968 Democratic convention, sitting there with my father and my mother, and my father getting really upset as the police swung their batons at the student protesters outside the convention hall, beating the demonstrators down. At one point he bolted up and made reference to the police, visibly upset and angered. It came out in the ensuing hours and years that he had experienced a lot of police brutality growing up and that seeing the Chicago events had been a flashback for him. That night my father, the ex-Marine, and I were both appalled and in agreement about the incorrect actions of the police. On that event we bonded politically and in a sense historically. I saw then that different people's experiences, while maybe not exactly the same, could become a shared experience that can allow people to open up to one another; that a shared experience could open a door that could allow different people a chance to work together to improve our quality of life for example. We didn't always have to be the one whose experiences were too unique to be shared. I began to file those in the back of my head as a collective history and experience, to be used in the future.

By the time I was in high school, I was in a pretty good situation, especially compared to others I knew. I often think of how lucky I was to be born when I was, for I went into high school knowing I was going to college, knowing I wanted to study political science and to be a part of the positive social changes of the future, whatever that might be. At the same time that I'm thinking that, in East LA, the blowout and the Chicano moratorium were taking place. The blowout was when Chicano students walked out of the classrooms at Lincoln High School demanding that they be given a proper and solid education, and respect. These were youth that knew they weren't being prepared properly for college and they took action. Again, I was the benefactor of good fortune and some luck. My school was relatively progressive, or perhaps it was that I had some good teachers, but I was also very aware of how fortunate I was to be where I was. When I learned that just a few miles west there were students who were not being properly educated and prepared for the challenges we'd be facing soon enough, it sunk in. I began to understand that I was in a position many people my age and class were not and maybe I could use this opportunity to help effect positive change in both the civic and social process, to the benefit of those whom I saw as the isolated outsiders.

I think, in part, because I grew up watching and reading about the Kennedys, I was inspired to believe that I, too, could be a part of such a story: "Outsiders grow up and help make change." When I was young, I was attracted to Bobby Kennedy's belief system. He felt that those of us who were privileged enough to be educated should be the ones helping others who weren't so privileged. He inspired me. For whatever reason, I don't know why, I had this sort of inner fortitude that drove me. Despite the fact that some people around my hometown were trying to cut me down or imply that, as a Mexican, that's not what you can do, or should do, or are even supposed to do, I had this strange kind of optimism or belief that people can stand up and make changes, and that people can do things that they are "not supposed" to do. Not a blind optimism either. More of a pragmatic form of hope.

There are certain points in some people's life when things are just completely taken out of their hands. Like my father: One day the U.S. government drafts him and plucks him out of the hills of San Diego and he's a Marine. He had no choice in the matter. If he'd been born a few years earlier or later, maybe he wouldn't have gone into World War II, but he did. It became a pivotal point in his life. Because I did have some breaks in my life (I didn't get drafted into Vietnam; I received a good education), I wanted to take advantage of them. It's a privilege that I graduated from high school in 1971. There were many working-class kids who found opportunities opening to them that they may not have found or had ten years before. I was a little naïve maybe, a little bit optimistic maybe, but also there was a part of me that said "I want to do this, this is what I want to be like and here I have the chance." I have been able, to a large degree, to live the life I've wanted, not as it was dictated to me. So when I say I was lucky, I mean in the sense that I figured that out early enough, and appreciated it enough, to want to try and use my advantage in a positive, and not a selfish, way.

I'm also lucky in that I had those days and nights under the arbor where those stories of hardship and success were related, and that I was just smart enough to absorb them. To be able to put together all that information and figure out that there are some people who've had to do tough things just to survive, and that's all they get. And that there are others who get to do many of the things they want to do and can ask the question, "How do I get to the point where I can do the things I want, in the way that I want, and be able to dictate what my life is going to be like as much as possible, and not be stuck doing what I have to do to survive?" I was just naïve and strong enough not to be pulled down by the naysayers, by those on many sides who might well have suggested to me that I should not dream too large.

After college, I worked different jobs, took classes for learning's sake, traveled, and tried to learn from my experiences. I was gaining practical political science training through my work experiences. I'd wanted to teach, but when I graduated from USC I felt I wasn't ready or prepared to teach. Not so much in terms of subject matter as in terms of having experienced life and its trials. Eventually I went back to school and received my teaching credential and taught for eight years. For me this was a great opportunity to put something back into my community and society, and I really enjoyed it. However, I reached a point in my teaching experience where I worried that perhaps I wasn't doing a good enough job. This was something I went through at the end of every semester and academic year, but one particular day I was truly frustrated and I walked out of the social studies building to get some air when I saw one of my fellow teachers, Liz Hicks, walking by. About a month before her husband, Joe Hicks, had been sworn in as the executive director of the Human Relations Commission for the city of Los Angeles, and on this day I just looked up at her and blurted out, "Are there any more positions open?" I'd heard him say that they would need five project coordinators to work the city on the night of his installation, and she stopped, laughed, and said to me, "You know, I was thinking about telling you about that, but I was afraid that if you took it, they would get mad at me for you leaving." To which I responded, "Let's talk." The end of the story is that within a month Joe and I had spoken, I'd interviewed, and he'd offered me the position. Now remember, since I was very young I've wanted to be involved in government, and to try and be in a position where I could help communities like the one I'd grown up in. To be offered this opportunity was a dream come true for me.

While I felt that teaching had allowed me to help contribute and put something back into our collective society, and I loved teaching, I'd also talked all my life about civic engagement and the need to be a part of the solution. I saw an opportunity for me to move into an arena where I felt I could be good and effective. Here was my chance to work with communities similar to my old neighborhood and with those that often never had the opportunities we experienced. It was time to put my money where my mouth was, and to face the challenges I'd often dreamed of facing as a youth. As a child I remember decisions being made that affected communities even as many in those very same communities felt that they were being left out of that very process. I learned then that there were many different ways of being a part of that process. One way was to teach. Another way was working inside the governmental process, and once there, working to change some of the perceptions of how government and community work, or don't work, together. Quite frankly, as I studied U.S. history and government, I saw that the power elite was a very narrow group of people. By elite I mean those individuals who get the higher levels of education, who receive the tools needed to be the ones who are running things, making the decisions that affect our lives, whether that's government or industry. Or the educators, for that matter, who give out the "proper" social norms of our society. I told my students that they needed to understand that for many in the past, education had been, for the most part, about teaching the accepted social norms to immigrants, working-class communities, etc., and not necessarily about teaching them the tools to think outside the box, to make decisions on their own, or to open the doors of perception—to, therefore, change the way we look at our society and ourselves.

That's how I looked at government, as an agent for those communities with limited tools at their disposal. An agent that could help provide avenues for communities who felt disconnected from their government and the decisions being made that affect their lives. In partnership. I am, after all, a product of the Kennedy era, which gave us a different twist on what government and civic involvement could be and how it could look. Looking back with today's standards, a lot of people might say that they didn't do all that much, but at the time what they stood for, real or not, was, I think, pretty earth shattering. It was the new frontier. They supported civil rights, as best they could. They asked us to get involved. That is one way many of us from that era who are now involved in local government got the activist bug. Some of us where I work now will sometimes look at each other and say, "You know, twenty years ago we probably wouldn't be here." I'm speaking about those communities in particular who were a part of or affected by the civil rights movement: women, African Americans, Chicano/Latina/os, Asian Americans, Dust Bowl migrants, and so on. Someone who looked like or fit into those categories most likely wouldn't have been given some of the opportunities that we are being given right now in the not so distant past. This is very important because other outsiders need to be able to see examples of people who are different than the norm and say, "You know what, if that person can do the job and it doesn't matter what their ethnic background is, or class origins are, etc., maybe we can too." I saw this job as an opportunity to be able to help change some perceptions about those who work within the governmental system, of how government works, or doesn't, and of helping change some ways that government and the community interact. I think government should be there to help and lead when needed—not dominate—and to help give the tools out for civic engagement as they are needed.

I know I've had a run of good luck to some degree, even though it's been a lot of hard work too. Once again, luck is being prepared and being at the right place at the right time, so I wanted to take advantage of that. Also I thought I was good at understanding civic engagement, and as a kid I guess I saw myself helping to continue that sort of "outsider thing" that I saw the Kennedys, Dr. King, Medgar Evers, Cesar Chavez, and others like Barbara Jordan and Gloria Steinem being a part of. People who became leaders, who were pushing the envelope, speaking up for a lot of other people in need of being heard. But I also see other people down the line who can be a part of this engagement, who are also trying to do civic actions. Writers, artists, as well as people in government, educators, others trying to shake the tree and say, "Look, there are a lot of things out here we should take advantage of!" Encouraging others in those neighborhoods around LA, around the country, where leaders lie fallow because no one has encouraged them to become a part of the process. That's one of the reasons I wanted to get into government.

I had to face up to the fact that one of my strengths is that I have an understanding of politics and government. In my 20s I was often confronted with that point, that if you go into government you are selling out. Damned if you do, damned if you don't. As if somehow sitting off to the side and being self-righteousness in one's analysis, while never being directly involved, somehow makes you better. It reminds me of a Woody Allen scene where a playwright is bragging that he has never had a play produced, although he'd written a play a year for the past twenty years. To which his friend comments that it's because he's a genius. Because both common people and intellectuals find his work completely conflicting and incoherent proves he's a genius! I came to see that my fear of failure may have been holding me back from getting more deeply involved in trying to effect some change in the attitude of and towards government. Sort of, "better to condemn than to try and move the process and fail." Well, it's a bit like that for some people. You can criticize from afar, but if you go into government, you've sold out.

I had to come to terms with the fact that I do understand government and I have a bit of a knack for it, which is why I'm where I am now. That's not to take anything away from nonprofit or community-based organizations. We certainly need them. I hope that all local governance can someday be down to such grassroots levels that there'll be less of a need for larger government. They are on the front lines in many cases. Where I'm able to do a little piece of anarchy in my work and help out the grassroots of our city is when I'm able to bring names and numbers and information about grants and information about monies that are being offered out there to community organizations which might not otherwise get those pieces of information. Or might not get a program from city government in their neighborhood because they were unaware of its availability. Also in our work we can help to interconnect community-based organizations to other organizations with like-minded issues so they can assist one another in their work. I find myself every so often in a position to be able to help some of those organizations.

I think civic engagement is a multipronged attack. What we do at the Human

Relations Commission isn't just one person sitting up at the top looking down upon everything and bequeathing upon others because they were good little boys or girls. It's more along the lines of "We're all in this together and if we don't work together, if communities and people don't find ways to work together, we can all fall down together." If this happens, we're not going to progress as well, nor as far, or as best we could, or perhaps should, as a society.

I'd love to work for a nonprofit or community-based organization at some point. This situation just happened to be the opportunity that popped up for me. I looked over at it and I said to myself, "I've been in a school district, I've dealt with the school bureaucracy and I know that there are highs and lows dealing with such a large monolith. I'm not blind to that. However I've always wanted to be part of a solution, so if all I do is sit back and yell and scream at government but never take an active role in trying to transform it, then what have I done to help change those aspects that I am unhappy about?" So I seized this opportunity. While being a part of a nonprofit would most likely be viewed with better favor by some people, since it isn't government related, I think that both sides are a part of the overall civic process. One shouldn't necessarily think that government is inherently evil. If so, I'd ask "Why?" Government, after all, is supposed to be about the people, and those who don't get actively involved, I think, are sometimes one of our biggest problems. If we aren't involved someone else surely will be. And those who do get involved yet don't educate themselves about the many community issues and concerns that are out there, so they have a better sense of who they are working with—they too are a problem. They are supposed to be working for the many communities, not just *a* community. We have government for certain reasons, not the least of which is we can't seem to trust ourselves. Sometimes I feel as if we established governance so we could have someone else to blame when things go wrong.

What does, or should, public service mean to me? Well, in my life, in terms of me as an individual, I see public service and community service as a way to help extend civic engagement into local communities and neighborhoods. A way for public, private, and governmental sectors to begin working together, not against one another. This is transformational government. In Terry Gilliam's movie *Brazil,* a story of government run amok, the character Tuttle, who, Zorro-like, breaks bureaucratic red tape, keeps repeating the line "We're all in it together, kid!" Well, as I began to look at our society and the world at large I began to understand that for me, that is true: we are all in this together. It isn't about serving one group over another. We need to develop a community-wide view where we are all a part of a larger community while also being a part of a smaller entity. Public service can help develop that sense of civic engagement and leadership in our society. It can also kill it if done for selfish reasons. For me, one should be in public service for the right reasons. By that I mean you're there to help communities transform themselves, sometimes as *they* see fit, to help develop civic engagement, civic responsibility also, and not just because you want to get elected to an office. That may happen and be a part of the end result, and that can be good, but if one comes into this work with too narrow a vision, I fear they will turn off more people to public service and public visions than not. Or maybe even corrupt the process itself. For me, one good aspect of my job is the view that we're trying to work ourselves out of a job. If we can get others in more localized ways to deal with and take responsibility for the issues that we are currently mandated to work on, then there is no longer any need for us.

Public service means working with all community people across the board, not just those who are heard the most, or who have the best access to someone of importance. It means that all public servants should at least want to try their best at all times and in whatever they do. If they don't want to deal with communities and the hard issues therein, then don't take the position. The most obvious public servants that the public sees and deals with are local politicians, the fire department and police department, and teachers—those people who are on the high end of the visual spectrum. But for me public servants also includes that person who walks into city hall every day and sits down behind a desk and takes the public phone calls, does the filing, because they are often the first people the public comes in contact with. They are all a part of the larger process, part of the larger city services in this case, and in terms of my work, I can't make it without them. I need their assistance, as does the public. All of us need to see that we're also apart of the "we're all in this together" idea.

Public service can also be as simple as the individual walking down the street who sees a soda bottle lying there on the ground and takes care of it. You have helped your community in one small, but good way. It wasn't your bottle, but the community is yours and that's the larger picture, the civic engagement aspect if you will. Everyday little things, mundane things can lead all the way up to the big things. It's about thinking and saying we're a part of a larger whole. Since I'm taking from that well, I should try and put something back too. I'm not saying we're all going to have equal needs all the time, but it tends to equal out. In my work I see that many people are very concerned about their quality of life. People want clean streets, paved roads, the ability to get clean water, etc. Well, if we all put something back to help the collective so that it improves itself, whatever that improvement is, whatever form that takes, and not necessarily monetarily but in ways that allow everyone to be a part of this process, that improves us as human beings. Isn't that a good thing? Don't we all benefit in the long run? In order to achieve that, we need an environment that makes it safe for people to learn and live, that makes us feel a part of the whole and want to be a part of it. So, for me, public service is an everyday thing, or as they say in the vernacular of the day, it's 24/7. It's a lifestyle. If you're benefiting from our society, you should help out as best you can. But then that's the way I was raised. At a minimum I see public service is that those who are able to take the time and are able to put back into the well from which we are taking, to replenish it, should. And do so understanding that we'll all gain from it in the end.

In our work with the Human Relations Commission, we deal with inner group, interracial relations across the city. One of our goals is to find ways to engage people with one another, with the many others we have here in LA, as a way to dispel fears and break barriers. Instead of building new programs, we look for those programs already in existence, that already work with people from different groups and communities to cross lines and to work with one another. We then help to flesh out the human relations aspects of those programs and help to outreach the programs into areas not traditionally involved before, into neighborhoods and communities we've worked with and built relationships with over the past few years. We hope that this work will not only begin to build coalitions, but will begin to point out to folks that we do have some shared commonalties, things from which to build. These are points we try to point out whenever possible.

We have been moving toward a more proactive perspective in our work, asking "What are the things that we can do or the questions we can ask that will help communities become more civically engaged?" instead of completely projecting upon them. By asking and listening and working together, hopefully we can help community members become a part of the process of governing their own areas because, after all, isn't it better for all when they help do it? That they get involved and take responsibility instead of feeling unempowered. If we can help communities to become proactive, to keep an eye on things in their areas, to build relationships with others and use those relationships in a positive way, quite frankly, we might begin to change some negative views people have of government. You know, that "they come in, get their photographs, and then they disappear and you don't see them again until the next elections come around" syndrome.

That's essentially where we're at now, trying to branch out our work in collaborative ways, to be proactive, and to learn from our contacts as well. For example, one of my partners, Emily, is assigned to work with and advise the LAPD. She was certified in 2002 as an adjunct instructor at their academy. Her thing is to talk to them about issues of conflict, communication, and diversity—within the department and in the community—and how these issues affect their work: How they are dealing with people out in the communities they serve, and how they are, in turn, being perceived are critical aspects of their jobs. So she's actually out there teaching, adding the H.R. element to the training. She just taught an eight-hour course on conflict management that was required for every sworn and civilian employee, from clerk typists to deputy chiefs. She has also been doing role-plays with recruits in the areas of domestic violence, sexual assault, and mental illness. And she is even designing a curriculum on leadership to be taught to LAPD command staff.

Over the past two years we've also become involved in helping to facilitate community meetings across the city, including helping to facilitate some town hall meetings for the mayor's office, LAPD, and other city agencies. All of us in Human Relations have been very active with the Department of Neighborhood Empowerment (DONE) here in Los Angeles, which has become another of our collaborations, and whose job it is to help develop neighborhood councils across the city of LA. We've done facilitation work with many developing neighborhood councils across the city, work that has allowed us to learn a lot about the many different communities across Los Angeles.

Another one of my jobs is to, essentially, be an observer—to try and keep up with the shifts and moods across the city. We go to different meetings or local events, talk one-on-one with people, and get down and dirty in the communities they live in to hear the range of issues and thoughts that are out there. It helps us to try and access what may become hot topics of discussion citywide, or in a local area, or what may even just be the rumblings of a few. It helps us overall when we sit back and say to our supervisor "Well, this is going on here," or "What we're seeing here is." By bringing back observations and information from the many different areas of our city we are trying to piece together the current landscape of Los Angeles. What we gather may not be the complete picture on it's own of what's going on across the city, but it could be a piece of the puzzle.

I think of our work as transformational. The best example I can think of is my work as a facilitator working with some neighborhood group. There have been four or five places where I've walked in and the people I'm going to work with look nothing like me. Not just in terms of background, but also in terms of the community I came from. And in some cases they have been in parts of town that have been very closed, to be polite, to outsiders. I walk in and it's my job as a facilitator to try and not only get these two groups that may be at each others' throats at that moment to work together, but, to some degree, to get them to look at government a little bit different. Maybe more as a partner than an enemy. Then to have them look at me and say "Well you may look different but if you can do the job, if you have the right intent, then it doesn't really matter." I have a chance to break some boundary lines in my work, and I'm aware of that.

I think a lot of my friends who are in the outsider category themselves are aware of that because we discuss this every once in a while: The idea of how we can help transform the way people look at government, at themselves, and at other groups of people that they might not otherwise ever interact with. We're aware of that when we are out there and know that the way we act will be looked upon by the people we're working with as an example, right or wrong, of what government is or isn't. Now, when I'm able to go out in communities and take information and give people an opportunity to begin to find the tools that they need so they can help be involved in their own area, I think of that as transformational government. I'm not going out and dictating to them saying "Government is the only one who can do this for you." I'm actually going out and saying government is here to help, but you're also the government and you're the ones that may know best about your communities. But if you don't take the bull by the horns and get involved, well someone else will be making those decisions for you. I personally think that the more active people are in those lower levels, meaning virtually block-by-block, the more effective the change you can have locally and in terms of how you view your own community. You are also more dangerous to the higher echelons of power and government because those higher echelons can't as easily cut off those small clumps of people who have the tools and the will to be heard, and are able to say "this is what we need." They are essentially being what I think of as dangerous, which means they are being a positive presence for all, not just some, in that community, and are helping to take charge of things.

What I'm advocating when I go out and try to give people the information and the tools they need to be able to understand how the system works, is that this is an opportunity for them to be a part of the process. For us to work together to improve or maintain our quality of life here, for the larger community. To take responsibility and to work with the many others across the city, and for us too, in government, to go the extra mile as needed. Now, I think some people that I work with in the government system don't necessarily see it this way. Some see it like, "We'll dish this out and that out, and we'll do this and do that, but nothing more." Or "It's my job to do just this, and it's not to think about other things, or do things not on my job description." We in government need to make the extra effort, to be the example. What I'm able to do right now is to go the extra mile. I understand how to find out who does what within the city structure—what department do you have to call to pick up trash, what department do you have to call to take care of graffiti, what department do you have to call to find out about getting potholes fixed? I can then tell community people I work with how to access those services. That, if they take action, they can bring government to their neighborhood. That if they don't let ring the phone ten or twelve times or keep calling back they may not get the service they want. That those who call ten or twelve times often get what they want, for the most part, and they often happen to be the elite. The elite understand what it is you have to do to obtain results. Now when I say elite, it doesn't necessarily mean money-wise, but those who have the information and know-how to use it. I think it's easy for people and communities to feel lost and disconnected from big government. We can help, we should help, people to access services, just as we can and should learn and access information from them to help our work. Working together just might help to transform how people in our communities see or think about what government is or can be, and also what community is or can be.

Do I love doing this kind of work? Yes, I do. Do I enjoy myself? Yes, I do.

Would I miss it a little bit if I had to lose it? Yes, I would. But that's the ultimate end result: That those communities we work with become so truly diverse and inclusive, and really know what they need, that I have to transform myself to do something else work-wise. I don't want to be the one for all time who walks in saying "I'm the one that's going to take care of you. I'm the one that knows better." I want to be able to walk in and have them say, "You know what, this is what we want, this what we need, boom, boom, boom," and it honestly is for the best for all. It is about throwing a monkey wrench into government. The government is best when it's fresh and it's changing.

I believe in order to do good work, you have to have take care of yourself and rejuvenate because it is important to you as a person. Sometimes after work on a summer night, if the Dodgers are in town, I'll head on over to the ballpark and take in a game. I love to watch a ball game on a mid-week summer's night, sitting by myself, keeping score and just enjoy the solitude. It refreshes me. Other times I'll go to my local coffeehouse where I might run into people I know and start talking about all kinds of things, from the mundane to politics and government, local or internationally, and take from that energy that also refreshes me. In the mornings I also try to take a few moments for myself. If I didn't do it at home, I'll sit in my car for five minutes or so, turn the radio off, and just, for lack of a better term, meditate. Think. I'll think about the things I'm going to do, or want to do that day, or just relax. I also find visiting my family is an important well for me to take from. Dropping in on my mother, or visiting my cousin and her girls, or visiting friends. Because if you don't and you're overloading yourself in your work you just might not set a good example for your community folk. If you're not happy, it can affect the way you do your work. I have a tendency to run through the week working from 8:30 or 9:00 every morning to 7, 8, 9:00 at night, sometimes later depending on the meetings I may have, or the research I'm doing. I tend to do that Monday through Thursday, and I do have to work Friday nights occasionally and weekends as needed. But I also will find the time when I need it to relax and rest. My supervisor is always on us to not overextend ourselves, and I'm getting better at that. I do make time for myself, and every few weeks I'll just get away from it all and rest. In the end you just have to do that for yourself, and understand that it's not being selfish. It's just being good to yourself, and to your work.

I'm going to give this work the best I can give it. I'm going to run as hard as I can run until I can't run anymore. That's the driving force for me.

Part III

Transforming Institutions

Story

Transforming Bureaucracy

Douglas MacDonald, Secretary
Department of Transportation
State of Washington

When Cheryl first met Doug, he had been the secretary of the Washington State Department of Transportation (WSDOT) for only a short time. He was already making waves, working to transform a bureaucracy steeped in an "engineering mentality" into an active, citizen-centered agency. Transportation in Washington state is a place where the rubber meets the road with regard to citizen disconnection and discontent. For most Washington citizens, nary a day goes by when they do not encounter a transportation issue, whether it is funding, gridlock (on the I-5 corridor, specifically), or maintaining rural roads. Washington state citizens, like those in other states, encounter government in the form of transportation policies and problems on a daily basis. As a result, WSDOT is a place where citizen attitudes are formed and shaped.

As secretary, one of the first things Doug did was to move his administrative office from the top floor of the WSDOT building on the State Capital Campus to the first floor, signifying his availability to the public. In addition, he began to appear everywhere, in an orange WSDOT safety vest and his hard hat. At a major accident on I-90, Doug was the spokesperson for the media, not the department's public information officer. After a maintenance-related incident that resulted in unanticipated gridlock, Doug appeared on a Seattle radio talk show and admitted that WSDOT had made a mistake.

Doug came to this position after a successful run as the executive director of the Massachusetts Water Resources Authority (MWRA). Under his guidance, the MWRA transformed the management of the water supply and waste treatment systems for greater Boston. The key reasons for the success of this project, according to Doug, is that the project had a strong goal consensus; the broadest possible ownership of the project was encouraged; the work was grounded in management commitments linked to the values of transparency, collaboration, and respect and a commitment to quality and integrity; the project benefited from the delivery of a constant succession of benefits;

and the project was blessed with good timing and good luck. Doug brought all of these tendencies with him to his work with WSDOT.

Doug considers himself not so much a product of his Harvard education as a product of the Peace Corps.

> My university education is in the Peace Corps. That is my alma mater. I went into the Peace Corps being well suited to do what the Peace Corps did because I had a lot of interesting experiences in college that prepared me to do that sort of thing. But, I don't feel like I am a graduate of Harvard College and Harvard Law School. I feel I happened to go to those places to get educated, but that, in fact, the Peace Corps is where my class is, where my group is. When I went to the Peace Corps' twenty-fifth anniversary a few years ago, I felt it was the one place where the group with whom I self-identified was just like everybody else in the world, except on a whole set of value issues they are about one inch in a better place, collectively. That inch is only a little bit, but it is extremely important for me to see that I have had a series of experiences that affected me that were totally mainstream, totally predictable, totally conventional, and yet internally oriented just one inch away. The Peace Corps is a very important part of who I am because it symbolizes the ability to get out of one culture and think about life in terms of another culture. And so, quite a lot of my story would revolve around those themes.

Like others profiled in this book, Doug was influenced during his childhood by activist parents. His father was the first commissioner of the Washington State Commission Against Discrimination.

> My father is/was a prominent aggressive, radical attorney in Washington state. And in many respects, I am a product of some of his thinking, but I am a totally different personality. The reason is that my personality is not adversarial, and I reacted to the adversarialism of litigation and the angry contentious litigation model for problem solving and came out in a totally different place. If you ask what the word "collaborative" means to me, it is the opposite of litigation contentiousness. Collaboration suggests that you solve problems—you don't win. I am also extremely competitive and goal oriented. I'm not a laid-back person. So, you know . . . it's just that I'm in a different mode.

Doug took the job at WSDOT after nine years at MWRA. He needed a change, wanted to get out of Boston, and "this was an opportunity to come home, which was important in a psychological sense."

Early in his career, Doug had the opportunity to be mentored in a job by a wise and gifted director.

He had been a budget director in California. He knew a lot about a lot of things. And he was a model for me in the ability to have a significant public position and not allow it to distort your basic sense of values and your sense of self, including a sense of democratic perspective on what the whole game is about. It was an exciting agency to work in. He gathered around him a whole bunch of young and talented people. We were all liberated to do our thing. Looking back on it, he wasn't very old then. But he had the ability to just sit and watch a whole bunch of talented people work and get work out of them. And he never lost his sense of both perspective and humanity on what it was all about. That mentoring experience was very important to me because it set a model of how you behaved if you were boss. I don't think people get very good models in that respect. I never, then, imagined that I would one day be the boss; coming to be a boss happened kind of by accident. Once I did, I understood that is what I am. I have an easier time with it than I did ten or twelve years ago. We are all in this together; that is really important for people to fall back on. That is not inconsistent with knowing when and how you have to be strong and assertive, but you don't have to be a jerk to be a good leader. So much of what is going on in public life today has to do with the corruption of power in terms of people's personal sense of entitlements and not a set of responsibilities and accountabilities. A perfect illustration is the ethics laws on accepting gifts. Many of the material inducements of minor league corruption are being washed out of the system. But the fundamental power corruption in thinking that you are entitled is still at work. I got an invitation the other day to be at the VIP section of fireworks on Lake Union. There should be no VIP sections, and the heads of state agencies shouldn't be invited to such. It is fundamental, but nobody gets this. One compliment I was once paid—and I regard it as a really high compliment—is that I am a democrat with a small "d." This pleases me immensely because it seems to me that this is what one of the goals should be.

Doug defines public service as, simply put, "working for the people."

I would like to think that in your enterprise, you have created something that serves communitarian values or structure. A sewage treatment plant is a public service. Making pet rocks isn't. I'm not interested in making movies or selling cell phones. That is not public service. I'm not interested in making or selling cars. I am interested in making transportation systems. That is communitarian. Making sewage treatment plants is communitarian. Working in mental hospitals is communitarian. Education is communitarian. Those things happen because we have to do them together. We don't do them for a profit. I could have made a lot more money doing something else. But that doesn't matter because I get my compensation in a very different way. I've enjoyed the opportunity to create public service, especially the infrastructure business, which has enormous tangibility. When you build a sewage treatment plant, you are looking at very tangible structures. It's probably different if you are teaching sixth grade; you don't have the same tangibility. But what is common in both respects is that you are doing what people have to do to have a community. I am a staunch skeptic in my public persona and even a stauncher closet opponent of privatization of public service. It is not entirely politic to really wear your heart on your sleeve on those issues. But, I do not believe that the private sector should be providing public service. If you can't tell the difference between what the private sector does well and what the public sector does well, then you shouldn't be in this business.

Doug's philosophy of public service is shaped by his commitments to transparency and communication. These are important because, if you can't explain in "plain English what you are doing and offer justifications and rationales that are transparent to the people who are affected by the decision, you often end up making the wrong decisions."

Doug considers his work to be

intellectually, absolutely challenging. I am like a carpenter who has had to learn to use lots of different tools because you might be asked on a given day to make a bureau or to frame a roof or refinish an antique table. You do best if you've done some of those things. I came to this job with a lot of different skills from past experiences. But the range of issues that are dealt with in a place like this is just fascinating. You have to think everyday about the bigger picture of what you are trying to achieve. You have to make strategic choices about how you position people's efforts and energies and what you are going to try to do over the short and middle terms. You have to be prepared to read, listen carefully, and assimilate all kinds of different information. You have to be a sponge for data and information on a hundred different things. And so my work day to day is in large measure about organizing information in ways from which we can derive patterns from which we can orchestrate and work toward goals. I don't think of myself as a big people-oriented leader. [But] the thing I have been most pleased by here is the personal dynamic with the people I am working with has been very rich—people have wanted to work with the kind of leadership that I have been able to give. Somebody said to me, "Gee, it is great to have a working secretary," because I probably work as hard, or harder, than anyone else in the agency. I am here more hours and am more intensely engaged than anybody else. After people got used to the fact that this is just the way I am, people were pleased to have somebody be committed and pleased to have somebody care about things they care about. They were pleased there would be an openness about communication. There are a bunch of people here who are able to merge their values, even though they are different people, in order to work as hard as they have.

When asked to define what he means when he says he is "one inch" to the side of mainstream, Doug explained how we, as Americans, do not understand our relationship to nature and how we do not understand that there "is only one world and we all occupy it together." He says, "I am not a radical, but my reactions will always be affected by my skepticism about a lot of commonplace, but misguided, verities which to me are inconsistent with the experiences I have had, the places I've seen, and the things I have had the opportunities to experience. . . . An inch isn't so much that I can't pass." It is this inch—the ability to see things with new eyes—that makes Doug a transformative public servant.

Doug believes there is the potential for transformation in his work.

I think we are at the boundaries in this agency where transformational things ought to happen and have the potential for happening. And I think I have had a chance to touch things that are transforming. I think we've got a long way to go to be transformational in a sense of being able to claim success in pushing for our aspirations. I don't think that this institution could be really different in a transformational sense. But I think if you push it in the right directions that there can be transforming moments both for opportunities for doing things and for people. I think if you can do that, you are doing very well. For me, transformational would be like waking up in the morning in an organization like this and you would be breathing a slightly different mixture of air—the mixture of oxygen and hydrogen would change. And there would be quantum shifts. It would be different. You would really have everybody in the same place. I haven't done that. But I have seen moments. I have several metaphors that I have found very convenient in thinking about this. One is what is said to happen in an eight-oared racing shell when people have learned to row together. I don't even know what the word is for it, but it is supposed to be a moment when the boat just sort of lifts out of the water and starts to row itself. The boat is propelled by eight people and all of a sudden their rhythm and synchronization takes one small part of greater energy that produces a quantum jump in the ability of the boat to move through the water. There are moments when we catch it and when you see everybody in the room in synch, and that is a great feeling. For a moment you feel in rhythm. And that is what a transformational organization would be about. Another metaphor is that of the symphony. The leader, the conductor, is waving his hands and, if he is skillful, he is keeping the beat, queuing the trumpets, and the orchestra is playing together more effectively because of the conductor. But the conductor is not playing an instrument; the conductor is not making the music. If you had an organization that was in a truly transformational mode, the leader might look a little bit of the person with the baton, trying to queue the instruments. I like that metaphor. Sometimes that is how it feels when things are going well.

In Their Words
Douglas MacDonald

What lessons would you like to share with others who want to practice transformational public service?

1. Never stop learning: You'd better be reading because if you are not, you are in trouble. I think one of the most interesting things about people is how many people you meet who just give up thinking it is important to learn about things. They just stop. It is important that you have a mind that is open to new things. You don't want to just check out. What's the point?

2. Recognize that every job has its disappointments: Public organizations are made to be destroyed, and are made to fall apart, and anybody who has worked in the public sector has to look at this. It takes a carpenter to build a barn; any donkey can knock it down. If you are really committed and really invested, you push it slowly up the hill to slightly, inch-by-inch better places, and then it will come down. It is the inevitable way of organizations like these. How you prepare yourself for that emotionally and personally, I have no idea.

3. Don't expect recognition for your work; look for it elsewhere: No person in an organization ever is recognized by the organization in proportion to their own sense of what recognition should be. People have this huge need to be thanked or recognized, which can never be satisfied.

4. Walk the edges: I want to be a little bit crazy, a little bit unpredictable.

The most important thing I'm trying to do here goes back to communication. Whether it is called communication, collaboration, transparency, business accountability—it's all the same thing. It all boils down to the quality of the reciprocity of communication. This is where the orchestra metaphor breaks down, or proves not to be adequate because at least in relation to the audience, the feedback—applause—is not exchange.

Comment

Transforming Institutions

How do you develop confidence in a community, and in individuals, to speak, stand up for, to strive, to fight and to have hope? I think those are the key challenges. It's not so much what building you are going to build or what social program are you going to change. But it's the people part of it, the part that has people investing themselves to make a difference, to make a change and to see that hope. That's the difference. That's the challenge.

—Che Madyun
Holding Ground: The Rebirth of Dudley Street

At the heart, we believe, of practicing transformational public service is "doing your own work," by which we mean activities that are developmental, reflective, and lead to self-knowledge. This work is needed to be a conscious practitioner and public servant. In addition, as the old adage states, we should "think global and act locally." Part of doing one's own work is to be actively engaged in one's local setting. All work begins at home, however one defines this (organization, community, politically, or otherwise). For the purposes of our work here, we define home (local) as the individual situated in organizational settings. As such, our description/analysis is lacking because home/local means so much more than just the who we are in our working worlds. For our purposes, we focus on the individual within the organization.

Transformational public service takes place within public organizations (government or nongovernment). Therefore, doing our own work means taking into consideration not only our personal work and reflection, but also the organizations within which we practice and the greater democratic system within which public service is situated. Doing our own work means doing what needs to be done to advance the self, but it also means participating in and contributing to organizational and societal transformation and change.

We shape the organizing principles for this chapter from Robert B. Denhardt, Janet Vinzant Denhardt, and Maria P. Aristigueta (2002). In their germinal book on public sector organizational behavior, they define organizational behavior as the "study of how people behave in public organizations. Organizational behavior is concerned with how people act, their motivations, and how they interact with others [within social systems]" (p. 5). They differentiate organizational *behavior* from organizational *theory* in its focus on the "individual and group behavior, needs and perceptions" (pp. 5–6), not on the organization. Beginning with the organization as the starting point, organizational theory tends to define problems as organizational and to seek solutions at that level. While organizational behavior is also concerned with all aspects of organizations and management, "it does so from the perspective of *people*" (p. 6; emphasis in original). What makes their work unique in the organizational behavior literature is that they contextualize public organizational, group, and individual processes in governance in the public interest. In other words, public organizations (and the people within) are different from private organizations in that the work must be done in a manner that is "consistent with democratic values and the public interest. . . . Therefore, organizational behavior in the context of public management encompasses both the values inherent in a "people" perspective on organizations and the values that guide public service in democratic government" (p. 6).

Denhardt, Denhardt, and Aristigueta suggest that organizational behavior in the public interest is "the product of the complex interactions among individuals, groups, organizational factors and the public environment in which all this takes place" (p. 6). Taking this as our cue, we organize this chapter along three levels of analysis: individual and group; organizational; and the public environment.

Doing Your Own Work: Organizations

Evelyn Brom and Sheila Hargesheimer tell us, most poignantly, of the importance of doing work for organizational change. As they say:

> What we are trying to do that is transformational about this work is *how* we work. We are trying to apply our knowledge and experience of oppression and the practice of creating and sustaining nonhierarchical ways of doing the work learned in feminist organizations to highly bureaucratic, hierarchical structures. By functioning this way as much as possible, we challenge traditional structures. Everyone's voices and experiences and beliefs are heard, counted, valued, and incorporated. Everybody, regardless of position, race, and class, brings their voices to the work and this brings a high level of quality to the work. You have to work in this way for the dynamic between theory and practice to be real.

All of our profilees are doing work for organizational change. Doug MacDonald works tirelessly, no matter where he is, to flatten organizational hierarchies and to give voice to the already existing knowledge and experience of the workers at the Washington State Department of Transportation. By modeling risk-taking behavior and admitting to mistakes, he shows others in the organization (and citizens) that government organizations can, and should, be a site for change.

Joe Gray, as the following story shows, does his work to change governmental organizations both when he is employed by government and also as a consultant to government. As managers and leaders, all of our profilees practice a form of participatory, democratic management. They could, perhaps, be seen as taking their cues from James M. Kouzes and Barry Z. Pozner (1995), in their book *The Leadership Challenge.* Kouzes and Pozner suggest there are five leadership practices that can be followed by those willing to accept the leadership challenge. They include:

1. *Challenging the process:* Leaders encourage risk, innovation, and the exploration of new ideas and processes in themselves and others. They learn from both their successes and their mistakes.
2. *Inspiring a shared vision:* Leaders work with others to design visions that are inclusive and shared by all in the organization.
3. *Enabling others to act:* Leaders encourage, empower, and enable people to do what needs to be done. They work to get the processes, systems, and habits of the organization out of the way of the employees. They identify and facilitate resources to support people in their work. They promote teamwork, collaboration, and model the importance of these in their own work.
4. *Modeling the way:* Leaders are mentors and role models, doing their own work in order to practice consistency and integrity and model this work for others.
5. *Encourage the heart:* Leaders encourage and support others to do their very best and to act with good intentions. Leaders encourage others to do their work with love.

Doing one's own work, self and local, means working to transform the organizations within which we do our work. While individual transformation is essential, without the concomitant organizational work, transformation is temporary and is attached to the people practicing it. Our work must last beyond us; to this end, we are called upon to do our work both individually and organizationally.

Public Service Today: Transforming, Not Satisfying

We are in a particular historical moment in which our intentions toward governance and administering the public good tend to be focused on measuring "goodness" through efficient performance. For example, in January 2003 the Washington state House of Representatives unanimously passed a bill to require performance audits of all state agencies and functions as a response to citizens' call for greater accountability in government. The unanimity of this move was surprising; not one legislator looked beneath the surface of the accountability issue. Yes, citizens are asking for greater accountability, but are they asking for performance audits (superficial accountability) or for a deeper connection to and with government and the governance of civil society (deep accountability)? Will published performance audits reports satisfy citizen desires for accountability (one legislator is purported to have claimed that performance audit reports are not on the Book of the Month Club reading list), or is something deeper needed?

It may well be that citizens are calling for a deeper response from government. Nonetheless, performance audits are what they are getting. Performance audits as a response to a call for accountability reflects the contemporary orientation toward public service that is founded on the idea of the free market where good government is government that runs like a business and creates public value.

Much of the best thinking in the free market approach to public administration can be found in Mark Moore's (2000) work. Moore argues that the function of public managers is to use the authority granted to them, and the public funds they manage, to create public value. For Moore, the concept of public value has its roots in the private sector. In private sector organizations, managers are expected to deliver value to their shareholders in the form of greater profits. Moore contends that public sector managers have similar functions—they must deliver value as measured by the degree to which public endeavors use public funds judiciously and appropriately to serve the public good. For Moore, a public manager who creates public value does so by recognizing the institutional and legal parameters of her work, but innovates in ways that allow the public functions to grow and prosper to serve the public interest. Moore believes that public managers create value "in the sense of satisfying the desires of citizens and clients . . . through deploying money and authority entrusted to them and . . . establishing and operating an institution that meets citizens' (and their representatives') desires for properly ordered and productive public institutions" (p. 53).

We would take Moore's notion of public value one step further. As the people profiled in this book exemplify, the function of public managers, whether they practice their profession within or outside of government organizations, is not only to *satisfy* citizen needs and desires but also to *transform* them in the public interest. As O.C. McSwite (2002) indicates, to keep ourselves from falling into a potential viper's nest resulting from private sector practices thrust upon public enterprises, "we must turn our attention to ourselves and our life experience so far and find reference points for a new sense of personal meaning to emerge there . . . through *personally* grounded *social* concern" (p. 24; emphasis in original). Through this personally grounded social concern, transformation occurs. We are not necessarily talking about great leadership or doing great things, but about doing the daily, basic things mindfully and with commitment, compassion, and passion.

For example, in 1995 the Olympia (Washington) Fire Department (OFD) began to transform to its "value-added" practices. Using models developed in collaboration with like-minded fire departments, it transformed a militaristic, conflictual, command-and-control organization into a democratic, collaborative, and self-managed organization. Decisions are driven down to the lowest level and firefighters (called "members") are encouraged to "add value" according to their mission statement that, simply put, is: (1) prevent harm to people and property; (2) thrive organizationally and personally; and, (3) be nice whenever one can. In short, firefighters are encouraged to do their daily basic tasks mindfully with commitment, compassion, and passion.

While this organizational transformation has brought about significant changes for both the fire department and its employees, it also seems to have the potential to transform the citizenship of those touched by the department and its employees. Success stories show how firefighters are choosing to extend themselves, both within and outside of their organizational roles, to others. There are stories of an engine squad that built a wheelchair ramp for an elderly woman who broke her hip; an engine squad that cared for a hospitalized citizen's dog; an engine squad that cleaned and boarded up a demolished convenience store. While fire chief Larry Dibble says this is "satisfying customers," we pose that it is going beyond satisfying citizen expectations to *transforming* expectations. These firefighters are involved in activities that transform themselves as citizens and, potentially, transform those they touch. They are shaping and modeling active citizenship. They are doing what Frank Fischer says Robert Reich (1991) is asking of public servants. That is, public servants must do more than "simply seek to discover what people want for themselves and then attempt to find the most effective means of satisfying those wants" (Fischer, 2000, p. 227). Instead, public servants should "provide the public with alternative visions of what is desirable and possible, to stimulate discussion about them, to provoke reexaminations of premises and values, and thus to broaden the range of potential responses and deepen society's understanding of itself" (Reich, 1991, p. 9; cited in ibid.). Public servants, in this transformative model, do not rely on the way we did things in the past. They instead create spaces within which citizens rethink and reimagine what they believe and rethink and reimagine what it means to be a citizen (Barber, 1984; Reich, 1991).

At the core of the work of transformational public administrators is movement toward, as Denhardt and Denhardt (2003, p. 23) state, "building public institutions marked by integrity and responsiveness . . . with citizens at the forefront." At the center are democratic values of fairness, justice, representation, and participation. Transformational public service transforms both public service and citizenship beyond a simplistic notion of serving an individual into something bigger, a public interest that is shaped and bound by what Barber (1984) calls "we thinking" instead of "I thinking."

This work can, and should, be done in a variety of places. Traditionally, the public interest was seen as something static that came out of the legislative process; the role of public administrators was to implement the public interest as defined by elected officials. Under New Public Management reforms, the public interest is realized through market-like transactions and is the aggregate result of our individual behaviors and choices. In this model, there is no need for public administrators to worry about the public interest. As long as programs and services are managed efficiently and entrepreneurially and customers are satisfied, the public interest is served. The efficient and entrepreneurial management of public programs and services can be performed in any sector: government, nonprofit, or for profit. Therefore, the centrality of government as the "keeper" of the public interest is destabilized under New Public Management reforms.

From the Progressive Era until very recently, it was fairly easy to identify a public institution: public institutions were government institutions. While it was true that nonprofits served social welfare, advocacy, and other needs, they were seen more as a part of the pluralistic nature of politics than as public institutions (Lowi, 1979). Public institutions are not so easily identified today. Government is no longer the seat of public administration. Instead of one centrally located source of public power (government), there are now complex networks of micropower that permeate administrative life (Foucault, 1984). Serving the public interest is no longer the sole domain of governments (Light, 1999).

Therefore, the keeper of the public interest—especially a public interest that is based in shared values—is no longer only the job of government (Denhardt & Denhardt, 2003). Building on Deborah Stone's work (2001), Denhardt and Denhardt indicate that the public interest based on shared values "suggests a process that goes beyond the interplay of special interests to include shared democratic and constitutional values" (p. 73). While, "articulating and realizing the public interest is one of the primary reasons government exists" (p. 65), the roles governments play in governance have changed significantly in contemporary times. Government is merely one of many players that come to the table to articulate and realize the public interest; around the table are people from inside the government and those from outside the government. Both need each other to do their work.

Those on the inside of government need those on the outside to advocate and develop creative approaches that would be impossible to achieve within highly structured and bureaucratized governments. Advocates on the outside of government play an important role in helping citizens articulate the public interest, facilitating the coupling of interests, and realizing the public interest (implement, regulate, watchdog). Indeed, it is in these places, according to Fischer (2000), where "feminist, antinuclear, gay, environmental, and other citizen movements have increasingly turned to culturally oriented politics concerned more about the social and political *questions* asked than the *answers* per se. The politics of these new social movements offer, in short, a metacritique of existing institutions and practices" (p. 27).

Those on the outside of government need those on the inside to ensure that their work will endure beyond one project or organization; they need advocates working within to shift and change government processes and systems. Governing is much more than simply managing outsourcing contracts and collecting taxes. As Denhardt and Denhardt (2003) state, governments continue to play a central role in serving the public interest:

> In addition to its facilitating role, government also has a moral obligation to assure that any solutions that are generated through such processes are fully consistent with the norms of justice and fairness, and are arrived at through a process that is fully consistent with the norms and ethics of democracy. . . . In other words, the role of government will become one of assuring that the public interest predominates: that both the solutions themselves and the process by which solutions to public problems are developed are consistent with democratic norms and the values of justice, fairness and equity. (pp. 65–66)

Advocates on the inside of government and advocates on the outside share equally in the responsibility to assure the public interest predominates, as the people profiled in this book illustrate. Public service, no matter where it is practiced, can be a vehicle for justice and equity.

Transforming Institutions

Insider/Outsider

Joseph Gray, President
JEG Associated Consulting
Orlando, Florida

"It started with getting fired, which is I guess where a lot of stories start," says Joe Gray.

Joe continues:

> No, [my story] probably goes back further to my upbringing in a low-income family in a low-income neighborhood in the economically depressed city of East St. Louis, Illinois. Basically, I've spent my entire life engaged in public service on one end of the stick or the other. The first half of my life was on the receiving end. The second part of my life, or my adult life, has been spent mostly on the delivery end, either working in government or as a private consultant working with local government to provide services or resources to communities a lot like the ones that I grew up in.

We first met Joe when he was working for Orange County, Florida. Joe is one of the thirteen collaborators of *Government Is Us.* His chapter, coauthored by Linda Chapin, discusses a groundbreaking initiative in Orange County, as Joe explains:

> I started off mainly working in a social service delivery system in this conditional sense of providing services for families and youth in Orange County, Florida, but throughout my professional career I was always kind of a frustrated social worker or administrator based on my personal experience with the system. I got into this whole business because I always felt like things could be better and services could be delivered better than what they were. Government can do a better job of helping families to climb out of poverty and to really achieve some degree of self-sufficiency. After about fifteen years of doing it I realized that we were just chasing our tails. . . . Of all the

In Their Words
Joseph Gray

*What would you like to tell others about what it is like
to do the work you do?*

My firm does urban planning and community building. This covers a wide range of services including: land-use planning, community redevelopment plans and strategies, urban design, civic capacity building, economic development plans, and other related projects and services. Public involvement is my specialty. The primary service that we provide is connectivity between government planning bodies and community stakeholders. My primary customers are local government agencies (i.e., planning departments, CRAs, etc.). However, the primary beneficiaries of my work are citizens. I have built a solid reputation for developing plans that are generally embraced and supported by both my clients and my clients' clients—their constituents.

I love doing this work because it gives me an opportunity to make a living making a difference. I've spent the vast majority of my adult life in public service, working mostly in local government. I've also spent a considerable amount of time working in nonprofit, community-based organizations. I was mainly involved working within human service agencies, purportedly changing the life circumstances of the low-income families and individuals we served. There was little tolerance for innovation or creativity, and our customers (citizens) were viewed mostly as public service consumers with little input in the bureaucratic process.

Most of the work that I do now is related to community redevelopment project planning, which can be quite controversial and polarizing by its very nature. Urban redevelopment projects generally require the displacement (or relocation) of residents in economically distressed areas so that physical improvements such as new housing, commercial districts, and public infrastructure can occur. As one might imagine, the social and political implications are huge. Existing residents have genuine reason to be concerned about the displacement of existing tenants and the cultural gentrification of the area. Surrounding property owners are usually concerned about the potential negative impacts of redevelopment projects on their property values and "way of life" (traffic, commercial encroachment, etc.). Public administrators are usually anxious about things like the increased maintenance costs, liability, and staffing challenges presented by new public amenities, such as parks, pools, and bike paths. Elected officials worry about the political implications of this most public exercise.

As a facilitator of these planning processes, I have an opportunity to empower community stakeholders in distressed communities to improve their livability conditions and control the fate of their communities; interject innovative ideas and creative approaches into public agencies without dealing

(continued)

with the bureaucratic obstacles and political constraints that I had to deal with when I worked inside of government; build bridges of understanding between neighbors and neighborhoods; and impact public policy in a profound manner.

I work with community stakeholders and government officials to craft community revitalization strategies for mostly distressed communities. As a consultant, I am viewed as a nonthreatening assistant to public planners and administrators. I do the work that government employees loathe. . . . I work with citizens on their terms, meeting on evenings and weekends, translating complex planning concepts into lay language that normal people can understand. I then retranslate the ideas, priorities, and concerns of community stakeholders into the planning jargon necessary for government consumption.

In the end, all of the participants usually develop a greater understanding and appreciation of one another. Citizens have an opportunity to exercise influence over key decisions that affect their lives, and local government officials are able to channel public resources, consistent with community priorities. The capacity that is developed on both sides is self-sustaining in most cases. Empowered citizens become an asset to their communities and their local governments, often becoming more engaged in political and civic activities. Enlightened bureaucrats and elected officials become better public servants when they better understand the public that they serve. All of our communities become more livable places as community stakeholders and public servants work collaboratively to eliminate physical blight and strengthen the social fabric that clothes us all.

programs that have come down the pike, none of them were really making long-term sustainable differences in the lives of the families we were serving. We were helping people to pay a bill or to fix a window in their home or to deal with some immediate issue, but we really weren't moving people in the community forward.

In [the] Community Affairs [Department] I had the privilege of working with a really forward thinking county chairman who was interested, as I was, in taking the next step of building strong, stable, self-sustaining communities rather than band-aid approaches. We did some novel things here in county government. We started to look at what were those essential ingredients for improving livability conditions in communities, and it didn't take us long to realize after spending a lot of time out talking to folks in the community that the things that really made the difference in people's lives weren't the social programs that were given but, rather, those physical major life-sustaining kinds of things such as owning a home, and living in a stable safe neighborhood where you could raise your children to appreciate and to really want to reach for things. We took the department I was working in, the Community Affairs Department, that was administrating all the programs for needy families and added a neighborhood planning component. We brought over folks from the Planning Department and we started working with communities to put together comprehensive plans that went far beyond the social services scope to deal with the core issues of the community. We asked the question, "What does it take to create a livable environment for the community and at the same time address the needs of individual families of the communities?" We found out that it was everything; that you've got to deal with all of those key livability ingredients—things were like crime and safety and housing and parks and roads and sidewalks—in addition to the social needs. We started a program called the Targeted Community Initiative (TCI), where we target distressed communities throughout Orange County. Because we had the chairman behind this initiative, we were able to pull together resources from throughout county government and get all the departments to work together to address all those needs in those communities. Over a three- to five-year period, the county was able to make significant, targeted, investments in those communities, one at a time, rather than spreading those resources all over the county. We found that we made a huge impact.

Joe's work in Orange County was limited, as so often happens in public administration, by the realities of bureaucratic organizations and by politics. The first level of resistance was within the bureaucracy. People who had been doing things the same way for years resisted change. Because the people working to promote the Targeted Initiatives were able, with the chairman's support, to be effective—particularly because they were able to affect the budgets of departments and organizations that may have been reticent to cooperate—as Joe says, "we got a lot of resentment and the resentment built up over the three or four years that we were running the program." When the chairman was faced with term limits at the end of her second term, she became a lame duck and the people in the system who resented the work of the chairman, "circled the wagons around the front-running candidate." When the new chairman took office, the first thing he did was to call for the disbandment of Joe's department and the elimination of the Targeted Community Initiatives.

Joe continues:

As a result, I did what everybody does when they get fired: I started consulting with the intent that I was going to do that until I found a job. Because of the reputation of our work in Orange County, I found it relatively easy to find clients. I am basically taking the TCI concept of strong stakeholder engagement and coordinated and collaborative planning with community stakeholders and citizens. I was able to carve a niche basically going out and adding that element and working with larger planning firms as well as working independently with communities to develop real citizen- and community-driven redevelopment plans.

Joe differentiates between traditional community redevelopment planning and the kind of work he does. In traditional planning, experts develop a plan that they then take to the community for their approval. Typically, this planning process results in urban gentrification, displacing and replacing the existing communities and neighborhoods. In contrast, Joe

works with existing stakeholders to develop a plan for redeveloping the area with the understanding that there are going be some changes that are going to have an impact on folks economically, but you have to take into consideration where the people are starting. We can't build a house or apartment that will rent for $200 in today's market. So we build in safety nets along the way and, in doing so, create a project that allows those stakeholders to grow with the plan. If you go into this and you build in those safety nets and those measures that address the needs of the existing stakeholders at the same time you're addressing the physical conditions in the area, then you are able to rebuild an area and rebuild the folks with it by again taking those concepts we developed with the TCI process, that is, working with all the community stakeholders and service providers and utilizing community resources to help lift up the entire community and raise the tide, everybody with it, rather than going in and displacing everybody and bringing in a whole new set of folks.

Joe believes that he can only do this work outside of government; that, because of political and bureaucratic barriers, it is almost impossible within government.

It is ironic that I'm a lot more effective in changing the institution of government from the outside than from the inside. When you are inside the government you are a part of the bureaucracy; it is like being in the army, you know. You really are restricted in what input you have, you have basically a defined area of input and that is what people expect from you. As a consultant I get to work with the policy makers as well as the bureaucrats as well as the citizens. The way we work is the whole process is pretty transparent so those conversations that we have about things that work or don't work are put on the table and we are able to expose things without getting into trouble. Whereas, if these same concepts were being pushed from inside of government, . . . well when I worked for government, they got me fired. It is the policy and bureaucracy that stymied the creative process, and when you're outside of the bureaucracy you are free to be creative in the input that you provide to folks at the policy and administrative levels of the government.

I've done more with this—with the same ideas since I left government—than I was ever able to do within government, and it is received better. A big part of it is just exposure. You can have a good idea, but if it never sees the light of day it is not going to change anything. Unfortunately, in government it is easy to get caught up in that rut of doing things because that is the way you do them because there's no pressure with any government itself to be creative. You don't get any; there's no profit motive, there's nothing that drives creativity within government. Outside of government you can drive that creativity and have a much louder and more effective voice especially if you are channeling that voice through the citizenry. It's not me, Joe Gray, saying these things or presenting these ideas. These are ideas that basically bubbled up from citizens when all you do is facilitate the circumstances to allow those ideas to be expressed and to be communicated to the folks that need to hear them. [When] you go to work in government you are just going to a job, but you're impacting people's lives. I think those folks whose lives are being impacted should have the stronger voice in how you impact their lives. Government could be more effective if it were to look outside of itself for ideas and were more open to those ideas. Public servants need to understand that they don't have to have all the answers, that they just have to have the right questions.

It will come as no surprise to learn that Joe defines public service very broadly, to encompass any work that is done for the benefit of the general public. He believes we should be more focused on the notion of service to the public, and less on serving bureaucracies and institutions. As he said, we get caught up in our departments and agencies and "forget that it is really all about serving. . . . If you really have joy in your heart for serving, you are going to be an effective public servant." He is very clear that public servants serve from a variety of venues, both within and outside of traditional government institutions.

When asked what calls him to his work, he returns to his roots. In his youth, he watched people suffer and knew that the only way he was going to make an impact—the only way black people were going to make an impact for black people—was through government. Like the others profiled here, he grew up in the era of Johnson and Kennedy and was inspired by their work.

He believes his work to empower communities is transformational because it lives on long after he leaves. As he says:

Once you go in and empower communities, they don't become un-empowered. Once you go in and really create a situation where you engage citizens in working with their government, then government has to change because government is us, right? And if you start changing all the people that make up the other side of the counter, then those folks are going to demand a different

> level of service and accountability from government. This is what transforms government. An example: I got a call last week from the Orange County Planning Department requesting that my firm come and do neighborhood plans for them. They realized they can't do things the way they used to. It is not the same communities they were working in before. These communities are insisting upon being at the table. We transformed communities during our TCI work and that community is forcing a transformation on the county.

Like others, Joe's rewards are intrinsic and relational; seeing people and communities blossom and grow and hopefulness on the faces of people that were filled with despair and hopelessness. He loves the engagement with people he would probably not otherwise have occasion to talk with. He gets to be part of a community or neighborhood—with each project he arrives, in a way, home.

Joe works hard. This kind of work requires spending one's days doing the analytical work and one's evenings and weekends working in communities. His son is grown and his wife travels and works with him; they find they spend more time together now than they did when he was working in other environments. Joe stressed the importance of a partnership with another who understands and appreciates one's commitment to, and love for, one's work.

Joe recounts the days after he lost his job with Orange County as being some of the most difficult of his life.

> We went through a lot of despair, and the thing that got me through was being able to do this kind of work where, instead of focusing on myself and my own misery, I was able to go out and work with folks. I realized that there are a lot of folks struggling out there with problems more serious than mine. This work has really helped me grow as a person and it's humbled me because I see the real challenges that people are facing out there and I realize how fortunate I am to not have to deal with what people have to deal with every day just to get through the day.
>
> I've always been a fighter, and that's the problem for me. I was telling somebody the other day about how I had problems with almost every job in government and it was mainly because I was always pushing the envelope. It goes back to the reason that I was there. I never ever looked at it as just a job. To me it really was a calling from the beginning, and I was committed to making a difference. It was always frustrating for me to get in a position in government and realize that making a difference was not, necessarily, the goal—that I was one of the few people who actually had that goal in mind. It was always a challenge for me and I never positioned myself to fit in. Even when I sometimes tried, I would always sabotage my own efforts by not being able to get past this whole ideology of wanting to see government as a change agent and not as just a provider of services or resources.

In Their Words

Joseph Gray

*What lessons would you like to share with others who want
to practice transformational public service?*

1. Encourage active partnerships with all community stakeholders to plan
   and implement public projects. Most redevelopment plans fail to materialize because they lack the support of community stakeholders. Bringing
   everybody to the table in a meaningful way can be a painstaking process,
   but the ideas, energy, and resources that can be harvested make the task
   worthwhile. While you may never achieve unanimous agreement on a
   course of action, stakeholders are more likely to ultimately support (or at
   least not oppose) a project if they feel they had an opportunity to have
   their say. The continued engagement of stakeholders throughout the implementation process is critical, particularly when it comes to long-range
   endeavors, such as community revitalization projects. Encourage and facilitate the development of vehicles to support ongoing civic engagement, such as advisory groups and neighborhood associations. Public
   leaders should also continuously look for opportunities to educate and
   inform stakeholders regarding public activities, projects, and issues. Most
   importantly, we practice transformational public leadership when we
   embrace all community stakeholders as true partners in our efforts to serve.

2. Adapt bureaucratic processes as necessary to align agency goals and delivery mechanisms with stakeholder interests and priorities. Public officials
   have to constantly remind themselves of their service mission. All too often
   bureaucratic process becomes the ends and not the means to an end. If we
   become slaves to process we sacrifice creativity and innovation and isolate
   ourselves from the communities we exist to serve. As the needs, aspirations, and priorities of public constituencies change we must reinvent our
   institutions to best serve the public interest.

3. Look outside of government for answers and resources to address con-
   stituency concerns. Encourage staff to look beyond prescribed processes
   and public resources to solve problems. We should know after a half century of failed efforts by government at all levels to eliminate urban slums
   and related social dysfunction (poverty, crime, homelessness, etc.) that
   government resources alone are insufficient to solve the myriad of problems that we face. However, over that same period of time, we have built
   up vast tangible and intangible resources outside of government that remain mostly unengaged in the ongoing effort to achieve goals that we all
   share. It has been my experience that community stakeholders from all
   segments of our society are ready and willing to participate, if we create
   the opportunity for them to participate in a meaningful and respectful
   manner as full partners.

Joe is sustained and animated by his work with stakeholders, whether they are neighbors, residents, or bankers and developers. As he says, "being part of that whole process of transformation in an area really, really gets my juices flowing."

You have to believe in something greater than yourself, and for me I really believe in my heart that God wants us all to be happy and to really look out for one another and I feel like I'm fulfilling that promise to God every day that I go and do this work. I would describe myself as a helper, as a carpenter that's really building something and in many cases rebuilding something. It's not just a physical thing. It's more than anything building faith and confidence and giving folks the strength to believe life is worth living. To me, life is beautiful and we're blessed to be on this little ball of dirt. And while I believe in God, I don't know what else is out there, but I know what we've got here is such a wonderful thing and we spend most of our time being depressed about it. I'm the person that's there to tell them it's okay, you know, look at it this way. It's like those pictures that when you look at them closely, you can't see anything. But pull them away slowly you see all these wonderful things. This is what I feel I do in the communities: just basically take that community and tilt it a certain way so that people can see the beauty in it and build on that.

IV

Transforming People

Comment

To Be of Use

To be of use

The people I love the best
jump into the work head first
without dallying in the shallows
and swim off with sure strokes almost out of sight.
They seem to become natives of that element,
the black sleek heads of seals
bouncing like half-submerged balls.

I love people who harness themselves, an ox to a heavy cart,
who pull like water buffalo, with massive patience,
who strain in the mud and the muck to move things forward,
who do what has to be done, again and again.

I want to be with the people who submerge
in the task, who go to the fields to harvest
and work in a row and pass the bags along,
who stand in the line and haul in their places,
who are not parlor generals and field deserters
but move in a common rhythm
when the food must come in or the fire be put out.

—Marge Piercy

One of our favorite fictional characters is the transformational public servant Dr. Larch, the physician in John Irving's novel *Cider House Rules* (1994). Set in a time before abortion was legal, Dr. Larch, a flawed and lovely man, runs an orphanage that also provides choices for women with unwanted pregnancies. Women arrive to give birth to their unwanted babies and to leave them for adoption, but many more women arrive, under cover of darkness and clouds, to terminate their pregnancies. Dr. Larch's protégé is a young orphan, Homer. Homer works by Dr. Larch's side during most of his life and becomes quite skilled in obstetrics and gynecology, though without the benefit of formal medical training. Through a series of illegal maneuvers, Dr. Larch gains medical credentials for Homer, with the plan that Homer will take over Dr. Larch's work.

Homer, however, has other plans. The novel recounts Homer's Odyssey-like journey away from the orphanage, struggling with his beliefs about abortion, learning painful life lessons about the necessity for such work, and his return to the orphanage. Dr. Larch's words to Homer—"Be of use, Homer . . . be of use"—follow him throughout his journey. He learns that being of use is essential and the "rules" that govern behavior in other settings may not apply when one must, in Marge Piercy's words, "pull like water buffalo, with massive patience, . . . strain in the mud and the muck to move things forward, . . . do what has to be done, again and again."

Throughout the stories of our profilees, the words of Dr. Larch and Marge Piercy ring loud: in essence, our practitioners remind us to be of use. They jump into the work, submerge themselves in the tasks (usually disassociating themselves from ego, because it is about the work, not about them), and strain in the muck to move things forward. They are not parlor generals or field deserters; they move in a common rhythm, doing what has to be done.

Doing What It Takes
to Be of Use

Randy Scott, Principal
ACCESS, Inc.
Olympia, Washington

Randy Scott describes himself as a butter knife, on the cutting edge of significant change in public policy. Although he has spent most of his adult life in public service, working for various governmental agencies—county, city, intergovernmental, state, and tribal—he is currently an independent consultant and lobbyist. His clients include a variety of government agencies and nonprofits. Randy crafts independence in his work, which allows him to do both his "paid" work for clients (through his government relations and public affairs firm—ACCESS) and his "unpaid" work as a member of the board of several important and influential American Indian organizations. He accomplishes his ends—being on the cutting edge of changing policy—by doing his work in many different places and many different venues. This is a pattern he has followed for most of his working life.

When I was working with Sam [Deloria], when a session came I would go on the city payroll. After the session, I would go back to work for Sam. We were having trouble keeping our organization [Commission on State Tribal Relations] funded, so I would do other work to make ends meet. The Bureau of Indian Affairs (BIA) apparently didn't like us doing what we were doing and it was affecting our funding. There was still an ethic in the bureau's mind that when a tribe wrote an ordinance or policy it had to come through a bureau process for approval. And we were telling folks, "If you want an ordinance or policy for intergovernmental relations, do your own work." We didn't try to tell them specifically what to think, or what the answer was to those problems, but here is how you address them. And by the way, your relationship with the bureau is an intergovernmental one. The decision on how you deal with that is how you develop your relationship with whoever your problem is with. We were trying to teach people process.

Randy speaks highly of those who mentored him throughout his life, many of whom are/were stalwarts in Indian County and others, like Wally Johnson, who worked in city government and taught him everything he knows about lobbying. He says he is who he is because of those who came before him and those who took the time to teach him: "Some of it comes from my family, and some of it came from people like Joe DeLaCruz, Mel Tonasket, Roger and Russell Jim, Sam Cagey, Cal Peters, Lucy Covington, some of the long-time tribal leaders of this state. Most of those people are gone now. I learned from the best."

Randy's grandfather was chief of his Gitxsan clan, or house group, from the time he was a young man until he passed away. Randy spent a great deal of time with his grandparents in northcentral British Columbia as he was growing up. Randy's grandfather and other elders of his family significantly influenced Randy, perhaps paving the way for the kind of work Randy does today—work that moves radical ideas through existing systems such that all parties are served while social change is enacted. Randy went to his grandfather's house after Randy had spent some time at Alcatraz during the American Indian occupation of the island in the late 1960s and early 1970s.

I was in my early 20s. It was a period of my life when I had been to Alcatraz during the occupation. It turned out that I was too young and naïve, maybe too idealistic, for what I saw and experienced at the island. It broke my heart in terms of the idealism of the people on the island. The effort was a long one and the nonresponse from the government was very disheartening. I left the island and was kind of mad at the world. I had some really great conversations with my grandfather. During another visit, we were talking about working in a non-Indian world. I knew that he had done things all of his life. He helped organize the union of the BC Indian chiefs back in the 1930s, and had been part of establishing the native brotherhood and the national chiefs organization when it was running. So I asked him about that, and he said "Well, let's go back to the beginning. . . . When the non-Indians first arrived on this shore, what happened?" I said, "Well, I have read my history books, and I know that when they first got here they were sick and they had lost a lot of their crew because of malnutrition, and kicking their butts wouldn't have been hard for us, but in lots of areas that didn't happen. Especially, on the northwest coast, I know that our people treated them well, welcomed them to our lands, taught them how to dry fish and dry berries and dry meat, and by the time they got home they were in better health than when they came to our shores." He said, "Well, what happened?" I said, "Well, they sent all of their descendants." I couldn't think of anything else. And he said, "No, really, what happened?" And I said, "I don't know what you mean." He said, "Well, just think about it for a second. They took the things from us. And did they leave us anything?" I said, "I don't know." He said, "Well, if you think about it for a minute, what they left us and gave to us was a steel blade. And if you look at what happened to our arts and our ability to carve and make tools after contact when we had a steel blade, our arts flourished beyond belief." And he said, "So what did we do? We took the best of what they had to offer and used it to the best of our ability for our needs and that is what we are supposed to do."

From him and others of his generation I learned our culture isn't going to go away, our culture is going to adapt. Our ways aren't going to go away, our ways are going to adapt. And if we go out and we intermingle and we learn and we work with folks, we don't bring everything home; we bring the best of what they have to offer, and we use that to the best of our ability to help our people.

Chiefs are chosen in the Gitxsan tradition based not necessarily upon familial line. Decisions are made on the qualities of a human being.

The ability to think creatively or critically, the ability to possess and utilize the knowledge base. I think when I go home, people look to me for things, but they look to me for the external stuff. What I know and what can I teach. Chiefs know about the land and how to protect the holdings. You know what is on our land as a chief, you know what families within our house group have utilized things historically. You know when the berry seasons are, you know the fishing time, you know the time to hunt within our territories. And you know how to go ask permission from other territories to utilize their territory for a specific purpose. Sometimes I will be someplace and I will think, and something will flash back from my grandfather or my grandmother showing me something. In our ways, the grandparents are the ones that have the patience and the knowledge and the time to devote to teaching the little ones.

For Randy, public service is about doing what needs to be done to further a public agenda, not to further private agendas. He says, "Governance is important to me—finding solutions to things in a public way." According to Randy, public service is:

Involvement for advancing the public good for the benefit of most, if not all. Sometimes in tribal settings, that is as difficult to deal with and pass forward as it is in counties and cities. I think the nature of governance and the nature of a jurisdiction and the nature of elected officials within those jurisdictions aren't drastically different. I have worked with sophisticated bodies like the city council or King County council, as well as what people would think aren't as sophisticated as Suquamish or Quinault or Colville [tribes in Washington state] tribal councils. Answers, solutions, are more important than sophistication or appearance of sophistication. But the games that are played and the attitudes that are exuded, the desires both on a personal and on a collective basis, are present in all forms of government. They are all similar. And convincing people of that is not the easiest job. I watched the tribal and the city councils go through the same steps over a different issue.

Tribes may think that the state of Washington doesn't really care about tribes. My attitude is "new issue, new day. Let's play and see what we can get out of it." The game, if you will, in dealing with legislative things is a pretty fair set of rules. You get the votes, you convince people. Get twenty-five votes in the Senate, and fifty votes in the House. That is what you need. And then when it hits the governor's desk, get it signed. Those are the simple rules. And they are the same for everybody.

I consider myself a salesman. I sell words and ideas that end up in state policy, or in the state budget. It is up to me to help convince both my client and the legislature that the words and ideas that are beneficial to my client are good public policy. If you think through intergovernmental relationships, the fact that we haven't had them, and that we are starting to exercise intergovernmental relationships by being involved in state policy, is a major sea change in the state tribal governance. It is new and people are both leery of it and excited about it. The nonnatives, meaning the legislature, want good information. They are hungry for good information relating to the tribes. I don't think the tribes really know this, but if we showed up in mass—not with just one lobbyist representing all of them or anything—but if we showed in mass and got our act together in relation to any issue that was of real concern to us, we would be the gorilla in the closet and all we have do is open this door and say this is what we want. We would get more accomplished than what anybody could ever imagine. The problem is that people, both in the legislative sense and in the tribal sense, aren't convinced of that yet. I am continually selling that as an idea. I don't think that you can look at governance in Washington state anymore without involving the tribes and the areas that are important to tribes.

When asked to reconcile the idealist young man who spent time at Alcatraz during the Indian occupation, and the salesman, as he thinks of himself today, Randy said:

I think human beings go through evolutionary processes. If you learn from the opportunities that come, you will grow. I don't think that I have necessarily lost that idealism. From a native perspective, coming together and heading towards the same endpoint is achievable. What disillusioned me at Alcatraz was that this wasn't happening—it was one-sided, all Indian, no significant nonnative or governmental attention was given. What I am doing now is trying to get us to work together. I get to help show people who aren't here and aren't involved in the intergovernmental relationship or the intergovernmental mechanism on a daily basis of what it means to change governance. It doesn't matter who is occupying the space of government. We start with letting people know that we care, and that maybe at some point, there will be other folks who will care too, who will say, "Let's go help."

When asked whether his work is transformational, Randy reflects on stories in native traditions of change agents, tricksters, or shape shifters. This spirit is usually embodied in an animal (raven, coyote); the spirit is usually paradoxical, both change agent and not. He notes that most, if not all native traditions, had beings that were the changer and that these beings are very important to their cultures. Randy does not see himself in this way.

I like to consider myself just somebody that is doing the part of which I am capable. Like the chiefs of my tribe, they took what the Creator gave them and used it to the best of their ability. They evolved into it. In that sense, their development was organic. I interact with lots of tribes. I go to a number of the national meetings just to see where things are at and to make sure that I am still thinking in the right ways as it relates to various issues. I am trying to help our communities, in essence, truly become self-determined. I think because, generally, I am talking to nonnative people and they all relate to the Declaration of Independence, the Constitution, and the formation of the states and the states' constitutions, that I can connect the concept of home rule that is applied to everybody but the tribes. There has always been this idea that federal policy has to govern the tribes. What I am trying to do is help figure out ways for us to believe in our communities and teach the world that we are capable of governing, and that we are able to do it in spite of various policies that exist. Through the kind of work we do on an intergovernmental basis we can grow that, as well as we can learn from our mistakes. The policy that we work on this year in a state, two years from now we might learn that if we took it here or we took it there, it is going to be better, so we come back and work on that policy a little more. That is the accepted norm when it comes to cities and counties and sewer districts and water districts, etc. And it is yet to be an accepted norm when it comes to the tribal-state relationship. And that's what I want.

In his life and through his various roles, Randy has spanned a number of boundaries, crossing back and forth when needed to get the work done. When asked about whether that is problematic for him, he replied:

Sometimes it is confusing, and sometimes I think I couldn't have planned it any better. I can go back to the Association of Counties—go to their annual meeting and be on their agenda—and I have credibility because they know

me. I never planned that. I have the ability to share with them some thoughts
from tribal country in Washington state as it relates to counties and help them
understand that. In addition, I can go back to the tribes and say when I was at
the Association of Counties I learned this. I think everything I do and am able
to accomplish is based upon relationships. I don't think that anybody can be
effective in a legislative arena over the long haul without developing relationships and having the opportunity to prove one's credibility. Credibility comes
from longevity and from being in front of a committee, being under fire over
an issue, and someone asking you a question that you don't know, and you
say "Well gee, I don't know that but I know where to get the answer and I
will be back to you by 'x' date." And you have the answer to them by that
date. It is being able to argue. I have done both—argued in a nice way and
argued in a not nice way with people in an open committee of hearings and
at the end of the hearing stand up and say, "The issue made me hot. I know
it made you hot. Let's go sit down and talk about it." And being able to sit
down and talk about it creates a friendship and a relationship so that you can
then go forward together and work on solving problems. It is being able to
do those kinds of things, both for the benefit of the work that you do, but as
well for the benefit of what you might do in the future. I have learned a lot
by the school of hard knocks.

The whole idea is accomplishing something that is a change and can be
viewed as an advancement of policy, whether it is just changing one word or
changing an idea that the policy can only work this way. Changing so that
policy advances a little bit—that excites me: the idea of making a contribution
that can advance things or make things better. In the governmental work between the city and the counties and the state, we did lots of those kinds of
things that were just small, little changes. Most of the legislation that passes in
any one session, 90 percent of it is that—the small little changes that aren't
earth shattering, but they make all the difference.

When asked how the public policy process could be improved from what
can be learned from tribal governments, Randy declared:

In tribal ways, every issue has its time. You don't force things. Things aren't
bipartisan; they are family- and community-related. Whether families are active or not, they are still based upon the older clan or traditional structures. In
a community, something my grandfather said to your grandfather could be as
real as the issue of the moment in the room. And so it is that same way in the
legislature. Something somebody from my district said to somebody from
your district thirty years ago can be real in the room at that moment. Issues
aren't really forced in any country. You try to find the time and have the cour-
tesy to find the time in which people are ready to make good decisions.

A former speaker of the Washington state House, Joe King, said that being involved in the legislative process is a contact sport. You can't stay on your side of the net and expect things to happen. And I wholeheartedly agree with that. It is also true in Indian country, but it is a contact of sharing information rather than convincing. And so I think that sorting out that difference is fairly easy and I am comfortable doing that. I have had the pleasure and also the displeasure of being in rooms where I am the only minority person, or person of color, and when it is my turn to speak, I am usually one of the last to speak and I try to be the one that ends up bringing the room to the real point. And I think I am decent at doing that, of cutting to the chase, as they say. And I do the same thing in Indian country.

Randy understands the importance of playing the game according to the way the game is played in the legislative or the administrative arena. At the same time he is bridging the gaps and doing so with heart and good intentions such that he is able to contribute to making change. When asked whether he was seen as "selling out," as a player, he talked about a situation where negotiating a policy may have affected the ability of the tribes to take legal action, one of the formative policy tools for tribes. He responded to his detractors by saying:

What you have is an ability to work through the process, and if the process doesn't work now, you can sue with specificity [as opposed to suing for lack of action]. Some folks have called me an "apple"—red on the outside, white on the inside. I have got a thick skin. I know that at that point in time it was a good move. If I take work away from lawyers, I don't care. In my heart of hearts, I would rather have elected officials talking to elected officials to solve problems rather than going to a third party like a court to solve our problems. While there are times when one does need to use more formal legal means to get things done, often it's about helping other people learn to do things differently. I learned this through doing the intergovernmental work that I had been doing and helping develop the training programs through the American Indiana Law Center that we did on the Commission of State Tribal Relations. The speaker of Rhode Island was one of our commissioners at the time. Speaker Manning had significant concerns and, most likely, was against an Indian land-claim issue in his state. We asked him to become a member of this commission, and made him a co-chair of the commission along with Joe DeLaCruz (then chairman of the National Tribal Chairmans Association and president of the Quinault Indian Nation). By the end of the first year, he was saying "How do we solve the problem? I understand better." They solved a gigantic problem in Rhode Island, and it was because speaker Manning came to learn. When I saw that from start to finish, I was convinced with the idea that you can take a set of facts, and if you are consistent with your facts and your facts are true, you can love people to death with it to where eventually they will open their minds and hearts and start seeing things. And you do it in that matter—of loving them with it. You don't spoon feed them, you don't cram it down their throats. You just keep reiterating and being consistent. And people start learning.

<u>Comment</u>

Making Meaning
Doing Your Own Work

*Everyone is tested by life, but only a few extract
strength and wisdom from their most trying
experiences. They're the ones we call leaders.*

—Warren G. Bennis and Robert J. Thomas
Geeks and Geezers

Theory in Practice

In this section we explore what it means to put theory into practice—or, as
the title of this book states, to view portraits of theory *in* practice. We believe
the perspective of theory in practice is especially important given the debates
over the past several decades about whether public administration separates
theory from practice, divorces practice from theory, or is just plain atheoretical
(see, e.g., Adams & White, 1994).

At some levels, given the rules of the academy, the discussion of theory and
practice is essential to the development of public administration as an academic discipline. And we also know that many practitioners often view theory
as irrelevant to their daily work, as in "That's all well and good in theory, but in
my job I have to (fill in the blank)." This dichotomy reminds us of the intellectual compartmentalization of politics and administration, or of the seeming
incompatibility of democracy and efficiency. As the Green Party slogan states,
"This is what democracy looks like." It looks like all of the above.

What we hope to show is a glimpse of what it might be like to reflect one's
theory of transformation in one's practice, not in an idealized way, but with
the challenges and messiness and rewards and successes intact. There are
many lessons to be learned from these transformational public servants. We
do not expect each reader to take the same things from this book. Indeed, we
hope that each of you will come to your own conclusions. Our interpretations of these stories are not the only ones possible. In the tradition of
storytelling, and in the postmodern context of the death of the author and the

rise of local narratives, it is not up to the storytellers to interpret the stories for the listeners; this is the task of the listeners. The storyteller provides the container; the listener decides what to put in that container.

Practicing Critical Theory

What is clearest to us is that the individuals profiled in this book are practicing critical theories. In review, critical theory, as we see it, is a tapestry woven of several theoretical traditions, including the critical theory of the Frankfurt school, which focus on exposing and deconstructing the hegemonic practices that get in the way of substantive democracy and equality. Doing so often means speaking truth to power, something that all of our participants practice, often daily.

But critical theory can also be about not speaking when silence is more effective, or when silence offers the means for parting previously installed curtains of segregation, separation, and difference. We use the image of parting curtains, rather than tearing down walls, because we believe this metaphor is more representative of Gramsci's vision. Gramsci described hegemony as filling any available space in civil society. Power is both centralized in the political system and diffused across civil institutions. Consent is organized, and power is exercised, not just through official political practices and policies, but also in civil society, where many aspects of social and political identity are fundamentally grounded (Carroll & Ratner, 1994). Therefore, as our profilees show, institutions and practices must be challenged from both within and without. Change can only be achieved dialectically; if simple domination does not work, neither does simple protest or even simple revolution.

Consciousness, for Gramsci, is the product of practical activity and active engagement with the world. Gramsci (1971, p. 367) referred to this reflective process and resultant transition to political awareness as "catharsis." The cathartic episode is a first stage toward "further progressive self-consciousness in which theory and practice will finally be one (p. 333; see also Fontana, 1993).

This is why we suggest, through our profilees, that critical theory can be, and must be, practiced in our everyday lives. Essential to this practice is a decentering of the ego and the self by moving beyond the internal barriers that separate us from others and that keep us in fear of "the other." A decentered ego allows practitioners of critical theory to see themselves as facilitators, in Frank Fischer's (2000) words, not as experts. Practitioners of critical theory lead deeply relational lives. Practicing critical theory often comes out of life experiences of marginalization and, in turn, can make one feel marginalized, though perhaps in a more conscious manner. Therefore, central to the capacity to practice critical theory is a commitment to doing the work needed to take care of one's self and others. It also means doing the hard psychological and emotional/physical work that leads to personal growth and development.

After hearing their stories, we believe these transformational public servants share the following common elements—each is further developed subsequently.

- They are deeply passionate about their work. They work hard; they are not likely to win awards for achieving so-called balance between their work and the rest of their lives but they think about balance all the time.
- They tend to be, organizationally and personally, what Debra E. Meyerson (2001) calls "tempered radicals," serving as either reformers or change agents in their practices (Moyer et al., 2002).
- They are flexible, moving in and out of roles throughout their lifetime as well as moving in and out of organizational and institutional arrangements. The work is the point; whatever it takes to get it done, wherever they can.
- They bridge theory and practice. They do not believe practice is effective without the consciousness, reflection and the capacity that theory brings to understand situations beyond the personal. When situations affect us personally—when we cannot aggregate up from the personal to the political or the system level—we are locked into passivity or paralysis. Overcoming quiescence requires the ability to deconstruct the ossified "truths" that are offered to us and then reconstruct things in ways that better serve others and ourselves.
- They take a systemic approach to their work, working to change the conditions of everyday life and the institutions within which they work so that they are more egalitarian, democratic, and cooperative in the sense that power and knowledge are shared.
- They are lifelong learners. They never stopped learning after finishing formal schooling. Indeed, learning is part of what they do to find balance, often taking sabbaticals for the purpose of expanding and increasing their knowledge and experience.
- Influential figures play an important role in the lives of our profilees, including family members, world leaders, and mentors. They understand the importance of leadership, including that provided by both formal and informal leaders, such as parents and other loved ones, who deeply affect us. They know they are leaders and act accordingly, in all areas of their lives.
- They are deeply relational; their work and their rewards come out of relationships.

- They all have had life experiences that challenge them in one form or another, sometimes very painfully (what Bennis & Thomas, 2002b, call "crucible experiences"). They have the capacity to walk the "in-betweens" of self and other.
- These life experiences lead them to a belief that those who live the problem best know the solutions. As a result, they are all committed to participatory practice, something Gary De La Rosa calls a "pragmatic form of hope."
- For many reasons, they are not motivated by or for themselves. As a result, they can stand aside and let their work stand alone. They have strong self-esteem and quiet confidence (which they developed over time and often in reaction to their crucible experiences). They take risks, share knowledge and power, admit their mistakes, and color outside the lines. They are, by necessity, thick-skinned. Yet, even with thick skin, decentered egos, and strong self-esteem, they suffer and often emerge from situations bruised and tattered.
- They are deeply aware of the importance of doing the work needed to take care of themselves and others.

In the next sections, we expand on some of the elements listed above.

Tempered Radicals: Rebels, Reformers, and Change Agents

One way to think about the types of practice exhibited by our participants is to consider that public service can be approached from one of three perspectives: (1) as an idealist radical, (2) a "tempered radical" (Meyerson, 2001), or (3) a traditionalist (see Table 1).

A traditionalist is one who approaches public service from a noncritical perspective. Traditionalists work within existing structures from an incremental, or evolutionary, approach. They seek to change things slowly; they typically see change not as a radical construct. This is not to say that traditionalists do not have good intentions or good aims; many traditionalists seek to make important and needed changes in administration and policy. Their approach, however, is one of conformity, not of revolution.

At the other end of the continuum are idealists radicals. Idealist radicals are typically not found in traditional public administration institutions—they are usually found on the outside, in academic or in other nongovernment organizations. Idealist radicals are often social activists, working toward radical social change. They believe in revolutionary approaches toward social change and have little patience with incremental or evolutionary methods.

Tempered radicals are somewhere in the middle, sharing parts of their orientation with both groups. Idealist radicals and tempered radicals share

Table 1

Types of Practice

	Idealist radicals	Tempered radicals	Traditionalists
Revolution	Typically	Not usually	Not usually
Evolution	Not usually	Typically	Typically

Source: Loosely adapted from Meyerson (2001).

an orientation (ontology) toward radical change. Idealist radicals, however, have a revolutionary approach toward their work; they believe in bringing down the wall all at once. Like traditionalists, tempered radicals have an evolutionary approach toward their work; they believe the wall comes down brick by brick, or by parting curtains, to use the metaphor more closely aligned with Gramsci. Where they differ from traditionalists is the degree to which they accept the status quo and in their orientation toward radical change. They may also differ with regard to where and how they practice their craft. Traditionalists are more likely to rely upon familiar and extant political and administrative structures and processes. Tempered radicals are more likely to work outside traditional institutions and/or to use traditional political and administrative structures and processes as a means for transformation. Tempered radicals approach their work dialectically. As stated earlier, they know that simple domination does not work and that protest or revolution is not enough. Tempered radicals practice in the in-between of revolution and domination.

Tempered radicals can be found both within and outside of government organizations. According to Meyerson (2001, pp. 5–6), "tempered radicals are people who operate on a fault line. They are organizational insiders who contribute and succeed in their jobs. At the same time, they are treated as outsiders because they represent ideals or agendas that are somehow at odds with the dominant culture. . . . They are constantly pulled in opposing directions: toward conformity and toward rebellion."

Public servants walk a fine line—they are citizens, yet still accountable to the citizenry. Tempered radicals are public servants that walk an even finer line; who identify with and are committed to their organizations and institutions yet who also consider themselves part of, or allied with, some group, cause, or ideology that is fundamentally different from (and possibly at odds with) the dominant culture of their organization/institution.

Tempered radicals recognize and experience tensions and contradictions between the status quo and its alternatives. Sociologically, these persons exhibit ambivalence. Ambivalence involves expression of both sides of a dualism, in contrast to compromise, which seeks a middle ground and therefore may lose the essence of both (all) sides. In an ambivalent stance, the clear positions of the oppositions are retained.

Drawing upon Bill Moyer and his coauthors' (2002) theory of social change movements and participants, tempered radicals tend to move in and out of three roles: rebel, reformer, and change agent. The movement action plan (MAP) model of organizing social activities/social movements describes the evolution of movements in eight stages; shows how movements have incremental progress and successes (as well as setbacks); helps movements situate their work in the "grand strategy of effective social movements—participatory democracy" (p. 5); and elucidates and illuminates four roles of activism: (1) citizen, (2) rebel, (3) reformer, and (4) change agent. The citizen role encompasses generalist work as citizen activists, rebels put the issue on the social and political agenda by making the conflict visible, and change agents work behind the scenes organizing, enabling, and nurturing others to become involved in the democratic process. According to Moyer and his coauthors (2002), "the change agent's goal, therefore, is to help create an open, public, democratic and dialectic process in which all segments of society are engaged in resolving social problems" (p. 25). Finally, the reformer works to convert alternatives into new laws, policies, and practices via society's appropriate political, legal, social, and economic institutions using political and legal strategies. Reformers act as power brokers between the mainstream and the movement. While effective activists play all four roles competently, most of us will lean toward one or another of these roles in most of our work.

Contemporary examples of public servants (elected officials) playing multiple roles are the mayors of San Francisco and New Paltz, New York, who, in the early months of 2004, performed same-sex weddings. These officials, who probably typically act as change agents or reformers in their elected roles, took on the role of rebel in order to push the issue further on the social and cultural agenda and make more visible the conflict between conservatives and progressives on this issue. The same was true of the Multahomah County (Portland, Oregon) officials who used their positions to work toward legalizing same-sex marriages in their county. For all these officials, doing so was not without personal and professional costs, including indictments and recalls. Much is being written at this time about the civil disobedience of these officials, a paradoxical phrase given that the officials have disobeyed not in their roles as citizens, but in their official capacities.

All of our participants are tempered radicals and, as such, struggle with the tensions implicit in being pulled toward both rebellion and conformity. All of them are reformers or change agents, with a little bit of rebel thrown in. Across their life spans, each has moved in and out of these three roles.

Our participants also share a tendency to be boundary spanners, moving in and out of roles and institutions depending upon the needs of their work. All have worked in a variety of institutional arrangements: governmental and nongovernmental. No matter where they work, their focus is public service, as they define it. They recognize that social change requires that activists and change agents work both within governmental institutions and outside of government; they recognize that each is needed to support the other. The work of one is facilitated by the work of the other; neither is effective without the other.

The Importance of Others: Love, Care, and Connections

All of the profilees talked about the importance of others in their lives. Each was/is blessed with the presence of role models who helped shape a passion for, and commitment to, public service. For some, these role models are family members. For others, they are people in their communities.

Our participants also talked about the centrality of mentors who take them under their wings and teach them to be effective in their work. Much has been written in the organizational and community service literature about the importance of mentoring. Mentoring, done well and done organically—research indicates that assigned or required mentoring is less effective than the kind of mentoring that blossoms organically—may be the single most important thing we can do as transformational public servants. To use the title of a film from the 1990s, mentoring allows us to "pay it forward," sharing outward capacities and perspectives with the next generation.

Virtually all of our participants were significantly influenced by leaders of the 1960s and 1970s: John F. Kennedy, Robert F. Kennedy, Martin Luther King, Mahatma Gandhi, Cesar Chavez, and Gloria Steinem, among others. These leaders had a profound effect on how our profilees see the world and on their definitions of public service. Indeed, many of them said they would not be in public service were it not for the inspiration of these leaders.

The influence of social action leaders from the 1960s and 1970s is a reflection of the generation of our participants. Without intending to do so, we chose profilees who all grew up at about the same time. This makes sense as those who are in positions to practice critical public service, and to do so with relative ease, are those of us who are in our forties, fifties, and sixties. (It could also be argued that we, unconsciously, choose to profile practitioners who look just like us, the authors.) Regardless, the question remains: are the life experiences of the generation who came of age in the 1960s and 1970s so different from the life experiences of subsequent generations that the experiences and practices of one are useless to the other? Does this generation speak to other generations? If one was not raised in a similar time, is it possible to feel the same level of commitment to social change? Without experiencing the influence of role models such as those leading the women's, civil rights, and American Indian movements of that time in one's daily life, is it possible to feel the same passion about public service, particularly given that there is, apparently, a paucity of similar leaders today? As McSwite (2002, pp. 18–19) cogently stated, John Kennedy (and those like him) were able to "tap into an archetypal feeling of human community and call people to do something together in their own name. [Whereas, today] [George W.] Bush's call [is] for an invigorated citizenship whose hallmark [is] active participation in a healthy market economy, Kennedy's call was for a revitalized commitment to civic life through work in government, as public servants."

We know through our daily experiences as teachers of students of public administration that younger people are just as passionate and as committed to public service as are the generations that came before them. However, this passion and commitment is manifested in somewhat different ways. Instead of leaders like John Kennedy, Robert Kennedy, Martin Luther King, Mahatma Gandhi, and Cesar Chavez, we have Nelson Mandela, Mother Theresa, Magic Johnson, Bob Geldof, and Bono. Within ethnic groups, we have leaders like Rigoberta Menchú, Billy Frank, Joe DeLaCruz, Mel Tonasket, Bernie Whitebear, bell hooks, Wilma Mankiller, Winona LaDuke, Vandana Shiva, Haunani-Kay Trask, and the Reverend Al Sharpton who speak across differences. These contemporary leaders provide some relief from the relentless cacophony of voices calling for citizenship as a market phenomenon. They show us that it is possible to practice citizenship in a way that makes a difference in the lived experiences of others. And there are countless other leaders working in communities and on the streets, providing counter-messages to the citizen-as-consumer image.

Our participants also talk about the importance of relationships in their work and in their lives. Their ability to do their work is predicated upon the strength of their personal relationships, with lovers, partners, children, family, and friends. And they know the essence of their work is relationship with others—their colleagues and the people with whom they do their work. As Doug MacDonald says, "Our work is bound with webs of affection and respect."

These "webs of affection and respect" come out of care and connectedness and from the desire to counteract the individualistic pressures of our time—what Benjamin Barber calls "I thinking"—with something more connected and communal—Barber's (1984) notion of "We thinking." Erich Fromm believed that the deepest need of each human is to overcome separateness, "to leave the prison of his aloneness" (1976, p. 9). (Fromm wrote in the 1950s and his gendered language reflects that time.) He saw modernist humankind as fruitlessly searching for union through productive work, conformity, and orgiastic fusion (sex, drugs, violence, and the like). Fromm felt the answer to separateness is "in the achievement of interpersonal union, of fusion with another person, in *love*" (p. 17). He saw love as

> union under the conditions of preserving one's integrity, one's individuality. Love is an active power in man; a power which breaks through the walls which separate man from his fellow men, which unites him with others; love makes him overcome the sense of isolation and separateness, yet it permits him to be himself, to retain his integrity. . . . Love is an activity, not a passive affect; it is a "standing in," not a "falling for."
> (pp. 19–20)

Love is the capacity of a mature, productive character. The capacity to love is dependent upon one's culture. As Fromm says, "Love—brotherly love, motherly love, and erotic love—is a relatively rare phenomenon" in Western cultures (p. 75). Fromm saw that capitalistic culture alienates

> man from himself, his fellow man, and from nature. He has been transformed into a commodity, experiences his life forces as an investment which must bring him the maximum profit obtainable under existing market conditions. . . . Our civilization offers many palliatives which help people be consciously unaware of this aloneness: first of all the strict routine of bureaucratized, mechanical work, which helps people to remain unaware of their most fundamental human desires. . . . Man overcomes his unconscious despair by the routine of amusement, the passive consumption of sights and sounds offered by the amusement industry; furthermore by the satisfaction of buying ever new things, and soon exchanging them for others. (p. 78)

All of our participants are practicing a form of Fromm's notion of love. Whether they intend to do so or not, like those who inspired them, they are providing examples of being in the world that act as countervalences to the alienation of contemporary life. In doing so, our participants also offer counter-messages to the myriad messages of fear that shape our existences. As Jeffrey Rosen (2004, p. 10) states, our success in overcoming fear depends upon leaders that "challenge us to live with our uncertainties rather than catering to them. The greatest leaders of democracies in earlier wars did not pander to public fears; instead, they challenged citizens to transcend their self-involved anxieties, embracing ideals of liberty and justice larger than themselves."

To think about relationships as the places where folks get together to love one another, hold hands, and sing "Kumbaya" is a bit naïve. Relationships, even those built from love and respect, are not necessarily always places of harmony. James Hollis (1993) claims that the model of intimacy (relationship) that typifies our culture is one of fusion or togetherness. Relationships are not, according to Hollis, places for us to find magical others who may "save" us but, instead, places in which life attains its meaning. Relationships are containers for growth and development.

Another way of thinking about relationships and our relatedness to others is through Margaret Urban Walker's (1997) vision of ethical "practices of responsibility." According to Walker, practices of responsibility attempt to place people and responsibilities in context with respect to one another. She envisions morality as a social negotiation in real time, where members of a community work to refine understanding, extend consensus, and eliminate conflict. This cannot be accomplished, however, unless a community is in equilibrium—where equilibrium is present among people as well as within them. Such equilibriums coordinate beliefs, perceptions, expressions, actions, and responses. They are also reflective, critical, narrative, and grounded in analogy.

Critical reflection, which tests communal understanding of moral practices, pushes toward transparency, which Walker also values. Transparency is powerful because it exposes elaborate justifications and causes embarrassment, thus creating opportunities for transformation. Ideally, Walker (1997, p. 70) suggests, "moral accounts must make sense to those by whom, to whom, and . . . about whom they are given." Enhancing transparency encourages us as individuals to "see through the haze of habitual assumptions and our comfortable or uncomfortable familiarity with them in order to see what is actually going on" (p. 216). By pushing toward transparency, unequal, unfair, and exploitative practices are revealed.

Our profilees practice pushing toward transparency, whether it is through making agency information and work more accessible (and understandable) to citizens and, therefore, linking citizens to the power of information and knowledge, or through making processes and procedures transparent to that which lies beneath, for example, power, patriarchy, oppression, and exclusion.

Crucible Experiences

Each of our participants had experiences that significantly shaped their orientation toward the world, self, and others. These experiences came out of "difference" (race, gender, class, disability, sexual orientation, etc.), resulted from victimization, or came from an expansion of consciousness due to being exposed to other worlds and cultures.

As part of their work for their new book, *Geeks and Geezers* (2002a), an investigation of generational differences in leadership, Warren G. Bennis and Robert J. Thomas interviewed more than forty top leaders in business and the public sector. They were surprised to find that all of their interviewees, no matter what their age, were able to "point to intense, often traumatic, always unplanned experiences that had transformed them and had become the sources of their distinctive leadership abilities" (2002b, p. 40). Bennis and Thomas called the experiences "crucibles . . . after the vessels medieval alchemists used in their attempts to turn base metals into gold" (p. 40). The crucible experience "was a trial and a test, a point of deep self-reflection that forced them to question who they were and what mattered to them. It required them to examine their values, question their assumptions, hone their judgment. And, invariably, they emerged from the crucible stronger and more sure of themselves and their purposes—changed in some fundamental way" (p. 40).

Bennis and Thomas believe that great leaders possess four essential skills that allow them to find meaning in potentially debilitating experiences: (1) an ability to engage others in shared meaning, (2) a distinctive and compelling voice, (3) a sense of integrity, and (4) an adaptive capacity/applied creativity or, as they state, an "almost magical ability to transcend adversity, with all its attendant stresses, and to emerge stronger than before . . . composed of two primary qualities: the ability to grasp context, and hardiness . . . that [allow] a person to not only survive an ordeal, but to learn from it, and to emerge stronger, more engaged, and more committed than ever" (p. 45).

For Bennis and Thomas, these crucible experiences were the containers within which their participants transmuted the base elements of their experience (heavy, dark, leaden) into a positive experience that significantly shaped their capacities as leaders. The most common type of crucibles they document involve the experiences of prejudice or bias. Crucible experiences also often involve illness or violence. Most of our profilee's crucible experiences involved discrimination, prejudice, or violence linked to race, class, sex, or physical disability. This is not to say that this kind of crucible experience is essential for practicing transformational public service. However, it is likely that those who are most poised to practice this kind of work come out of traditionally marginalized communities or from experiencing the harmful results of unexamined assumptions about contemporary life. A crucial element of practicing transformational public service is an awareness of or an opening to how these experiences flavor public life and the ability to transform one's personal experiences into the alchemical gold of greater consciousness, awareness, and personal change: to emerge, as Bennis and Thomas (2002b) state, stronger and more sure of oneself and one's purposes. For our profilees, crucible experiences led to a perspective on public service that is transformative: a public service that is in service of the people.

Use of the ancient language of the alchemists is intriguing, especially as it relates to the work of the people profiled here. Alchemy is an ancient practice that flourished in Alexandria at the same time a school was developing in China. The movement was at its peak in the Middle Ages in Europe. Essentially and simplistically, alchemy is the attempt to transform base metals, such as lead, into silver or gold. Besides being a primitive form of chemistry, alchemy was also replete with a system of symbols that illustrated the alchemical process.

Alchemy is also an important metaphor in depth psychology. In Jung's view, the alchemical attempt to transmute base metals into gold actually represented a psychological process. The symbols used were representative of what he called the process of individuation. This involves a series of small, often seemingly insignificant changes in conscious attitudes and patterns of behavior. In this respect, it is important to note that the word "analysis" comes from the Greek *analyein*, which means "to dissolve." Analytic thinking in any context requires the dissolution of previously held "truths." In the context of self-knowledge, the analytic process involves the dissolution of various personae and the eventual reintegration of transformed elements. In this way, one can readily see the similarities between alchemy (dissolving base metals and transforming them into gold) and individuation (dissolving the persona and reintegrating into a transformed self).

Jung described four stages in the individuation process: confession, elucidation, education, and transformation. Confession, despite its possible religious connotations, is undertaken not for the purpose of absolution but as a means for recognizing (naming) contradictions. As we have noted elsewhere in this book, our culture does not value ambivalence. Indeed, there is often a certain kind of shame projected onto those who appear ambivalent: their reflection is frequently labeled laziness, indecision, or incompetence. Failure to meet societal expectations generates guilt; in order to alleviate guilt (a psychologically painful emotion), the individual often represses his or her most authentic observations in favor of maintaining the party line (so to speak).

Elucidation involves interpretation and integration of contradictions, or the conflicting messages one often receives. In organizational contexts, these contradictions are sometimes referred to as "espoused theories" versus "theories-in-use" (see Argyris & Schön, 1978). Individuals (and organizations) are generally aware of their espoused theories—these are the "rules" by which we claim to live and act. At some level, we are often aware of the discrepancies between what we say (our espoused theories) and what we do (our theories in use). The inability or unwillingness to reconcile these discrepancies tends to generate defensive mechanisms and routines that allow us to live with the contradictions, but in unhealthy ways. Rather than "confess" and analyze the situation, we expend a great deal of energy constructing compensatory behaviors: we rationalize, repress, regress, intellectualize, project blame, and generally do just about anything to avoid raising "messy" issues.

In the short run, this strategy can be maintained and may even appear to produce results. In the long term, however, ignoring contradictions becomes self-defeating. In organizational contexts, Chris Argyris and Donald A. Schön (1978) observed that such behavior leads to reduced levels of trust and commitment, along with a severely diminished capacity for change. Similarly, at the individual level, this kind of repression makes it impossible for persons to undertake education and transformation, the next stages of the process.

Education involves learning to integrate opposing ideas and energies. Perhaps not surprisingly, it involves both intellectual and embodied learning. Likewise, it can be both emotionally and physically uncomfortable, even painful. It involves coming to terms with the illusions we hold about ourselves, which we have used to shore up self-esteem and to maintain our sense of self.

Finally, deep change, or transformation, can begin. In this state of profound liminality, the individual recognizes both the old and new aspects of the personality. S/he feels transformed yet still deeply familiar, as in the crucible experiences spoken of earlier. When this change is also rooted in the musculature of the body, the transformation is, literally, visceral, akin to the muscle memory that athletes and musicians develop. This is the kind of transformation that critical theory envisions, also—a synthesis in which earlier elements are still present, yet different in an elemental way. Transformation is not the same as reconstruction. Transformation allows a transcendent function—the ability to be self-observant without being overly self-conscious or critical; to be knowledgeable about oneself without becoming inflated or dogmatic; to be stable, yet flexible, resisting the drift toward rigidity and ossification.

Decentering Ego and Democratizing Expertise

The crucible experiences of our participants led to a number of orientations toward their work, self and other that we believe are crucial to practicing critical theory. One of these is a decentered ego. Practicing critical theory requires that one put aside one's own needs for recognition and one's ambition. It also requires that we decenter the traditional notion of expertise.

Putting aside one's own needs for recognition and one's ambition is a tall order in contemporary Western cultures, particularly cultures where worth is measured through status and possessions. We are exhorted from an early age to have ambition. To make something of ourselves. To climb the ladder of career and material success. Yet, ambition often gets in the way of practicing critical theory.

It is not that one cannot ascend social, financial, and professional ladders as a critical practitioner; one's path, however, may be less direct and more convoluted than if one is a conformist. Still, critical practitioners are not likely to be rewarded with money and status, perhaps because these traditional rewards are less attractive to critical practitioners. These practitioners often seek, and receive, more intangible, relational rewards.

Central to ambition is ego. Ego, in Western cultures, is a controlling energy/drive. Our egos desperately want to believe that we are "in charge." As Parker Palmer (2000, p. 97) says, our ego wants to know "that we can make whatever kind of life we want, whenever we want it." He recounts a story: A Chinese child will ask, "How does a baby grow?" An American child will ask, "How do you make a baby?"

> From an early age, we absorb our culture's arrogant conviction that we manufacture everything, reducing the world to mere "raw material" that lacks all value until we impose our designs and labor on it. . . . We need to challenge and reform these distortions of culture and ego—reform them toward ways of thinking and doing and being that are rooted in respect for the living ecology of life. Unlike "raw material" on which we make all the demands, this ecology makes demands on us even as it sustains our lives. We are here not only to transform the world but also to be transformed. (p. 97)

An essential element of decentering ego is democratizing expertise. Our participants understand this; their roles are not to hold on to and parcel out their knowledge and capacities as their egos or ambitions see fit. They share knowledge and expertise. They practice forms of Fischer's (2003) notion of facilitation, rather than expertise, respecting the knowledge and expertise of others as well. They see their roles as the facilitators of process or, to use a fairly new term, as servant leaders. They are there to facilitate or to serve the needs of others, as an actively engaged participant in shared processes.

Democratizing expertise requires a significant departure from the trajectory of public administration and public service over the past century. The emergence in the twentieth century of the "knowledge society" has had consequences that were unanticipated by its initiators, many of whom (at least in the United States) were pragmatists and progressives. For them, science was to be the great equalizing force, contributing to the formation of a democratic community. The unexpected result, however, has been the creation of a knowledge elite increasingly concentrated in universities, corporations, and government (Bell, 1974; Gaventa, 1993; Merrifield, 1993).

Membership in this knowledge elite is, in a sense, by invitation only—extended through the conferring of degrees, the acquisition of professional credentials, or the securing of other forms of exclusive certification. Certain types of social controls govern the type of knowledge produced and for whom, through the organization of academic disciplines, the promulgation of professional standards, and incentives and reward structures for career advancement. Knowledge is transmitted through the publication of professional journals, participation in conferences, and membership in networks open only to those who are members of the club. Additionally, much of this knowledge is passed along in language that is unfamiliar to the uninitiated—the jargon employed by different fields (Ricci, 1984; Gaventa, 1993).

In this environment, the experts become the power brokers. By choosing to offer or withhold information, experts can manipulate the actions, or inactions, of others, controlling the emergence of issues in the public arena. When issues do emerge, these experts can exercise tremendous discretion over how they are defined (Lukes, 1974; Gaventa, 1980, 1993). The effect is frequently to declare as a "nonissue" many of the problems encountered by everyday citizens. Furthermore, because the knowledge of expertise is segregated into disciplines, little attention is given to the cumulative or interactive effects of related issues. John Gaventa (1993, p. 29) writes:

> Take, for instance, the case of a worker who is employed in a chemical plant, lives in a nearby community, eats and drinks the food and water from the land, and is dying of cancer. To gain a response from the system for action on the cause of the cancer, he or she will have to subdivide the problem into that derived from work, governed by the Occupational Safety and Health Administration or the Department of Labor; that derived from air pollution, governed by the air quality control board; that derived from water, governed by the Water Quality Control Board; that derived from toxins in the food, regulated by the Department of Agriculture; that derived from eating wildlife obtained through hunting, regulated by specialists in the Department of Fisheries and Wildlife; that derived from the consumption of other foods, regulated by the Consumer Protection Agency; and that derived from the interactive effects of them all—regulated by no one.

Expertise can be used to manipulate or perpetuate societal power relations. It can be used to "delay and defuse" an issue, as in doing a study that takes so long and produces such inconclusive results that the issue is abandoned. Expertise can be used to "impress and bemuse" (shock and awe?)—marshaling voluminous statistical evidence or sheer numbers of experts to overwhelm opponents. Finally, expertise can be used to "gloss and confuse" an issue, leading to political decisions based on somewhat arbitrary standards that are presented as scientifically (read: objectively) valid. An example is the acceptable mercury level for fish, which had been set at 0.5 ppm (parts per million) until 1977, when, after lobbying by the tuna-fishing industry, the "safe" level for mercury in fish doubled to 1 ppm (Merrifield, 1993, pp. 74–75).

Even more problematic is that, for the most part, knowledge experts are not accountable to those affected by the knowledge. This lack of accountability is rooted in the premise that scientific knowledge is superior because of its objectivity. Sharp distinctions are maintained between expertise—the study of a problem—and experience, or the subjective living of the problem. Experts may study the problems of poverty, homelessness, or inadequate prenatal care, but they must not experience these same problems, or identify with those who do, for fear of jeopardizing their objectivity. Information or knowledge that comes from personal experience is tainted with subjectivity and given little weight in official decision making because it is not scientific. Belief in the authority of expertise subordinates common sense, and in so doing subordinates common people.

In addition, there is great reluctance on the part of knowledge experts to share information with the public, out of concern that ordinary people will not understand the information or will use it for partisan purposes in a manner that threatens the experts' reputations for objectivity. Experts, like science itself, are supposed to be politically neutral. Having a professional obligation to describe only what is, and not what ought to be, allows the expert to abdicate responsibility for expressing opinions or taking remedial action.

Public administration and public service have been caught up in this culture of expertise, with detrimental effects. Public administration has become captivated by managerialism. The education and practice of public service professionals has become characterized by the mastery of instrumental analysis and technique, elevating process over purpose. The effect is to convince citizens that the substance of their concerns is unimportant, especially if those concerns cannot be expressed in the language of expertise. Administrators trained only in instrumental approaches and interpretations do not know how to question the effects of their actions on the lives of subordinate groups or to give weight to knowledge gained from lived experience.

By contrast, our participants are "on the streets" in a number of ways. They are willing to take risks and admit to mistakes. They share their knowledge and expertise. They honor the knowledge, experiences, and expertise of others. They have strong self-esteem, which they developed over time and often in reaction to their crucible experiences. They are, by necessity, thick-skinned.

Yet, they often feel alone, or marginalized, unmoored in a roiling sea. Strong connections with other practitioners of critical theory are essential; cultivating these connections is an important part of their work.

The Great Refusal

Part of the aloneness of being a practitioner of critical theory comes from the refusal to take part in the operations of the world as they are prescribed. Our participants are practicing, in a way, what Marcuse (1970) called the Great Refusal. Marcuse, according to Richard C. Box (2003, p. 257), did not intend refusal to be a social movement, but "the withdrawal of individuals from society in the interest of a 'pacified existence,'" refusing such taken-for-granted human qualities such as toughness, fear, obedience, and weakness.

Theorists in public administration, particularly David John Farmer (2003), have taken Marcuse's notion of refusal as a call for action, exhorting public administration practitioners and scholars to "become more self-consciously aware of [their] own relationship to power . . . and [to aspire to] thinking/practice that is radically multi-dimensional, radically human" (Farmer, 2003, p. 173). In other words, to refuse is to be a tempered radical, like Sheila Hargesheimer's mother who refused to accept cultural conventions and habits of mind as foregone conclusions. Her mother's self-efficacy and her sense that she could challenge norms and conventions allowed her to refuse to "act poor" and to pass that refusal on to her children. Refusers refuse to accept foregone conclusions and they believe they have the capacity to challenge (and eventually change) norms and conventions.

The personal and psychological costs of refusal cannot be underestimated. Those who choose to speak up are often punished (Alford, 2002). Archetypally, such individuals are scapegoats—those chosen to bear the burden of the sins of the collective and then banished into the wilderness to rid the collective of their sins. The term scapegoat originates in an ancient Hebrew annual rite where two goats are sacrificed to cleanse a community. One goat is dedicated to God (Yahweh) that He may pardon Israel and is killed as a sin-offering so its blood may cleanse and placate the angry God. The other goat, the expelled or escaped goat, is burdened with the sins of the Israelis and is sent out into the wilderness to "bear all their faults away with it to a desert place" (Perera, 1986, p. 17). The wandering goat is a sin-bearer, carrying the evils confessed over it away from the collective unconsciousness.

Each of our participants, at one time in his/her life, was cast in the role of scapegoat. The modern manifestation of the scapegoat phenomenon looks a bit like this: the scapegoat is usually a refuser or a tempered radical. In their refusal, refusers or tempered radicals expose the shadows and weaknesses of the people and organizations with which they are affiliated. If the refuser/ tempered radical is not in a position of power (and even if they are), it is fairly easy to project these shadows onto the scapegoat, personalizing the issue and, therefore, avoiding having to bring the darkness or shadows into the light. In other words, the scapegoat allows the collective to avoid dealing with the institutional problems. Banishing the scapegoat does two things: it shifts the center of attention away from the issue and it allows those remaining behind to continue to deny the presence of the shadow. The scapegoats carry the shadow projections of both individuals and the collective. It is a heavy burden to bear; many collapse under the weight. However, the scapegoat need not be seen as a negative archetype. It is possible to not internalize these projected shadows and, instead, to use the scapegoat complex as a way of serving the collective, as Perera (1986, p. 88) explains:

> Exiled scapegoats can, thus, return to serve the collective as agents of its deepest and most difficult needs. They serve by mediating the libido necessary to collective and individual life. But they are also a community unto themselves. They form a loose society of nonconformists. It is one devoted to the transpersonal processes underlying individuality and the secular collectives. Those in this society listen for the guidance that comes from the intersection of life and death, joy and pain, love and wounding. They are more or less willing to feel its paradoxical and raw nature. Since they struggle continually to accept that intersection in their own hearts, they can work with the inevitable shadow projections, not as a prelude to scapegoating and splitting in order to attach, but as a means of lifelong personal growth and ethical actions.

But, as C. Fred Alford (2002, pp. 131–35) notes, the route between the margin and the center is a two-way street. Those who refuse are often banished to the margins. Yet, as they are marginalized, "the power that moves [them] there makes a brief appearance at the center of society, reminding us of its existence" (p. 131). To the extent that practitioners of critical theory protect the space for refusal and contradiction, we postpone the one-dimensionality Marcuse feared.

In doing so, these practitioners are in what Buddhists call "the middle way," walking the razor's edge. As the Jungian analyst Robert Johnson states in his autobiography:

> Throughout my life, that middle place, when I can find it, has been an ecstatic place, a holy place. It's like a hurricane: if you can manage to stay in the middle, you will feel calm. Most people in the West don't believe

that the middle point is a solution; instead we want to do something. On many occasions I have advised a friend or a client: "Don't just do something, stand there!" Our Western heresy is most often an overstatement of doing at the expense of being . . . It is the brave and wise person who understands that he or she belongs right in the middle of a dilemma and that the solution is not to avoid it but to sit in the middle of the opposites and work through them. (Johnson & Ruhl, 1998, p. 50)

Depth psychologists have identified literally hundreds of archetypes. Caroline Myss (2001), for example, offers up archetypes that may ring true for transformational public servants, including the Advocate (lifelong devotion to championing the rights of others in the public arena), the Healer/ Wounded Healer (serves others by repairing the body, mind and spirit—usually expressed through channels other than Western medicine), and the Liberator (works to free individuals from entrenched beliefs and attitudes imposed from without). Again, this is because archetypes are the contents of the collective unconscious; innate, inherited patterns of psychological performance linked to instinct. Theoretically, archetypes are universal—humans in various cultures possess the same basic archetypal images—although our individual responses to them are entirely unique. We do not suggest these are the only images that may resonate for readers, although if they do, we encourage additional reading and learning, as part of one's personal work, in order to better understand one's reactions and responses to situations, especially stressful ones. This involves recognizing one's personal shadows, which we discuss next.

Embracing the Shadows: Doing Your Own Work

Practicing transformational public service is a tough job, regardless of how emancipating it can be for both the individual and the collective. Along the way, one must, necessarily, face one's own shadows—one must come face-to-face with him or herself. While our participants would probably say that they have approached this work to varying degrees, all of them have done a great deal of psychological, emotional, and spiritual work. Indeed, without this work, they would not be able to do what they do.

For Jung, the primary task of life was to learn to recognize, and come to terms with, those aspects of ourselves that contaminate our perceptions of others. Recognizing our weak or dark traits (our shadows, that which we often try to project onto others) helps us develop a fuller understanding of our interpersonal relations. This cyclical process, called synchronic individuation, requires us to continually mediate between our conscious and unconscious, appreciating the paradox and especially appreciating the discomfort it produces. Most people are not ready to begin the individuation process until sometime in midlife (according to Jung). Until then, we are typically too enmeshed in our parental complexes and our psyches are too influenced by the dominant culture around us (Young-Eisendrath, 1995). However, crucible experiences like those described above can be a catalyst for individuation.

It is hard to imagine, in our current pop-psychology world, that we would not be familiar with the notion of doing your own work or working on yourself. Opportunities to do so abound, some legitimate and others questionable. The point, here, is that *how* one does one's own work is less important than the doing it.

Doing your own work may mean pursuing traditional psychotherapy, with or without an intention toward the Jungian notion of individuation. It may mean pursuing a spiritual path. It may mean reading philosophy or the Great Books. It may mean immersing oneself in theory and other structural analyses. It may mean engaging in bodywork (yoga, dance, therapeutic massage, acupuncture, meditation, etc.). It may mean being part of a healing/recovery community. It may mean embracing the traditional path of your ancestors. It may mean going on self-renewal retreats and attending workshops. It may mean any or all of the above. The point is to do something.

As Lama Surya Das (2003, p. 10) says:

> Men and women who are in therapy are familiar with the phrase "working on yourself." When we do "work" on ourselves we are trying to become stronger, more accepting of ourselves, and more internally resilient. We are trying to further develop our mental health and well-being. The spiritual path is similarly filled with inner and outer work. The promise of transformation and even enlightenment exists, but only if we do the necessary work. . . . If we are paying attention and practicing some form of self-reflection, experience will gradually give us greater clarity and wisdom.

We are not advocating any one method or practice of inner and outer self-reflective work. Indeed, as one is resisting the domination of the dogmas of the past, one must also resist substituting a new dogma for the old. As we have said throughout this book, replacing old ideological systems with new ones that are just as dogmatic and require the same level of unthinking adherence to unbending principles is not the answer. There is something in the in-between. Find your in-betweens.

What you are likely to find on whatever paths you choose for your inner and outer work are startling similarities to the themes outlined in this book. Whether your choice is ancient philosophy or an ancient spiritual/embodied practice like yoga, you will find that the ancients speak remarkably clearly to us in these times. For example, a contemporary yoga text (Sell, 2003, pp. 18–20) has the following to say about pursuing a path to wakefulness:

> Being on a spiritual path, or living according to one's faith, means that a person aligns his/her self to a set of principles and values different than the everyday waking consciousness of our modern culture. Yoga philosophy asserts that we are also unaware of that essential truth, dreaming instead a self-centered fantasy that we think is real. Although we walk around and animate a life that seems real, in which we look and act awake, in terms of consciousness potential we are asleep and dreaming. We inhabit the Sleeping World. . . . A sense of pain and longing for union is inherent in the sleeping state itself. The longing is often so subtle and so dampened by the deafening roar of the Sleeping World's clamoring, that we no longer know that there is the greater possibility of conscious life awaiting us. In the spiritual world in which I participate, we often speak of *sadhana* [spiritual practice, in community] as a "work on self" or simply, "the Work." . . . Entering the Work is about exposing the myths of the Sleeping World and learning to listen to the whispers of longing for the real. The work involves enlarging our focus beyond our ego's limited viewpoint and into the larger context of spiritual life. . . . Awakening from the Sleeping World's dream involves having our mechanicality exposed to the light of awareness so that we can begin to chose a new way of relating to the world, to each other and to ourselves.

An essential part of doing your own work is knowing oneself. All of the profilees in this book have emphasized the importance of self-knowledge in doing their work. Again, self-knowledge can be pursued from a multitude of perspectives. From the perspective of depth psychology and critical theory, for example, self-knowledge involves a process, a practice, and a goal: the process of individuation and practice of holding contradictions moves one closer to the goal of wholeness and awareness.

Robert B. Denhardt and Maria P. Aristigeuta (1996) call self-awareness an *intrapersonal* skill. *Interpersonal* skills are those that facilitate our work with others and include communication, group process, conflict resolution, and other skills. *Interpersonal* skills are those that are applied between people. *Intrapersonal* skills, in contrast, are those that are applied within ourselves and include a "moral and psychological grounding" (Denhardt, Denhardt & Aristigueta, 2002, p. 23) that enables us to act with consistency and integrity. This is based on "a strong sense of self and the capacity to learn from experience and self-reflection" (ibid.). To become better at our work (and our life), we must learn about ourselves.

Doing this kind of work also helps with what has become known as the "battle of the sexes." An essential component of knowing oneself (individuation) is the process of coming to terms with one's contrasexuality—that is, our unconscious opposite-sexed personality. The contrasexual other both constrains and defines the self. As Polly Young-Eisendrath (1995, p. 24) says, "The way I act and imagine myself as a woman carries with it a tandem meaning of what I imagine to be male and masculine, what I see as human but 'not-woman.' . . . The same is true for the feminine other in the male psyche." Each sex carries envy, jealousy, idealization, and fear of the other sex, emotions that form intrapsychic barriers, especially when the two sexes interact. As long as we are working to overcome false dichotomies, it is probably long overdue to recognize that both sex and gender are socially constructed categories. It is time to begin to resolve this contradiction as well.

Individuation (self-knowledge) is an important process of psychological development for both women and men. But it is also a process of recognizing and understanding one's own contradictory nature, identifying and balancing the conscious and unconscious impulses. An individual must first learn to develop meta-cognitive abilities—the ability to think about one's thoughts, feelings, and states of being, looking at oneself through a third-person perspective, and engaging in a dialectical relationship with one's self. The personal awareness that comes through individuation permits disidentification with childhood complexes and a withdrawal of projects (Young-Eisendrath, 1995). In other words, knowing oneself allows one to be freed from the bonds of childhood complexes and reduces the chances that we will project our "stuff" outward, onto others.

Both interpersonal and intrapersonal skills are needed to practice transformational public service, as all our profilees tell us. One cannot exist without the other. In order to be effective in working with others, one needs to start with oneself. And, no person is an island (indeed, some believe there is no "I" without the "We"); it is through interaction with others that we come to know ourselves most fully.

A good place to start with the reflective and experiential work needed for self-knowledge is the organizational behavior text of Robert Denhardt, Janet Denhardt, and Maria Aristigueta (2002). Within are many tools one can use, including self-inventories, to begin the self-knowledge journey.

While we hesitate to suggest that transformational public service practitioners can be identified by a fixed set of attributes (deterministic thinking is not the point!), we find that our profilees do possess certain qualities that we would like to, hesitantly, present as "habits of heart/mind." We take this phrase originally from Tocqueville (habits of the heart was Tocqueville's expression for the mix of traits and mores that form the American character) through Robert Bellah and his coauthors (1985). Tocqueville believed that these habits of the heart, along with a strong inclination toward equality, were what was going to build a strong, democratic nation of people with relatively few differences in equality (economic, cultural, political, etc.). Bellah and his coauthors, like many other conscious social critics (e.g., see Cohen, 2001), found that Tocqueville's predictions did not play out because individualism overwhelmed equality and has, as Tocqueville also predicted, led to isolation, inequality, and the undermining of the conditions of freedom. Bellah and his collaborators offered a number of "habits of the heart" needed to counterbalance the rampant and dominant individualism. Our profilees also offer a number of habits of the heart/mind for those practicing or seeking to practice transformational public service. Cultivating these, it seems, is an important part of transformational public service.

Patience

As suggested by the social change literature (Moyer et al., 2002), change takes a long time to come, whether one is seeking individual, organizational, or societal/political change. Greg Coleridge said it well in his profile: One must be patient with the big things and look to accomplish the small things one can do in one's lifetime and be prepared to pass on the work to the next generation. He reminds us to take our cues from nature; change happens both incrementally and suddenly. We never know when a tipping point (Gladwell, 2002) will be reached and we cannot measure the degree to which our work contributes to that tipping point (just as, in nature, we cannot precisely know the events that lead up to sudden changes).

Tenacity

While being patient, one also has to be tenacious. Transformational public service requires that we work hard, perhaps for a lifetime, in the pursuit of our objectives. All of our profilees are examples here. All of them are committed, more or less, to doing a certain kind of work and to doing whatever it takes to do their work, including changing jobs or organizations and taking on the role of shape-shifters (tricksters, boundary-spanners; see Patterson, 2001), conforming to the shape of the situations, as Randy Scott in particular shows us, in order to get the work done. As Gary De La Rosa says, "I'm going to give this work the best I can give it. I'm going to run as hard as I can run until I can't run anymore." And, we think Evelyn Brom and

Sheila Hargesheimer embody tenacity in the deepest sense in their lifelong commitment to working to eradicate violence against women. Their work started at the individual level, both of them working in organizations that provide services to battered women and children. They moved into the public policy arena and are now trying to guide a major governmental organization (bureaucracy) toward shifting and changing the practices and perspectives that keep violence against women alive in our culture (patriarchy, sexual oppression, violence, homophobia, power, etc.).

Acceptance and Detachment

Doing this work requires that we balance our passions with acceptance and detachment. Acceptance and detachment do not mean passivity or apathy. Acceptance and detachment are active states of being where one is committed to the higher goal, so to speak, but not attached to how things play out on a daily basis (because it takes time and tenacious effort, and even with tenacity, we may not get to where we want to go in our lifetimes). Being attached to the fruits of our labor or to certain outcomes puts one at significant risk of burnout and despair; more often than not, the specific outcomes we envisioned will not be achieved. Attachment and nonacceptance also open the door for ego to drive our work (it ends up being about us) instead of the work driving our work (it is about the work).

Claire Mostel practices acceptance and detachment in her work as the Citizens Academy coordinator. She gets flack from all sides in her work; from citizens who are disconnected from and discontented with their government and from government employees who do not understand her work and feel threatened by the changes required of them. If Claire were attached, she could not have the necessary distance to continue to do the work in the face of opposition and discouragement. Joe Gray provides us with another example in his lack of attachment to being a county employee. When his work was disbanded in Orange County, Joe chose to leave the county in order to continue to practice his work. If he had been overly attached to his job (as opposed to his work), Joe may have chosen to stay with the county, effectively putting his work to an end. Making the move from a county employee to self-employment was a huge leap that required both faith and detachment.

Borrowing a phrase originally used in feminist literature (Haraway, 1991; Thornham, 1997) we suggest that practitioners of transformational public service practice *passionate detachment*. While this appears a paradox (and is), it is possible to be detached from something about which one is passionate. Here we take as our guide the wisdom of the ancient *Bhagavad Gita*. In it, Krishna tells Arjuna that acting with detachment means doing the right thing for its own sake, because it needs to be done (passion), without worrying about success or failure (detachment) (Kempton, 2004, p. 76).

Humility

Embedded in detachment is a sense of humility. This is also related to the notion of a decentered ego, discussed earlier. Humility is, perhaps, the most challenging of these attributes. The work is, ultimately, not about us. It is not about our ego or our ambition or about our rise to power. It is about the work. It is not about false humility as a mask for ego-attachment (for instance, seeking out praise and success but claiming humility as a way of feeding one's ego, but doing so in a "socially acceptable" way). It is about the self being less important than the work. This does not mean abandoning or sacrificing the self (a sure recipe for burnout, commonly known as the "caretaker syndrome"); indeed, this self knows that taking care of oneself is a primary element of humility. A hungry, bruised, tired, lonely, angry, hurting self cannot be humble, because it is clamoring for attention. Only an attended self can be quiet enough for humility. As Randy Scott said to us when we first approached him to be part of this book, "it's not about me, it's about the work."

Generosity

Implicit in humility is generosity or love. Generosity is a curious phenomenon. Confucius is said to have claimed that generosity is one of the five elements of perfect virtue, the others being gravity, sincerity, earnestness, and kindness. Generosity implies a willingness to share unselfishly. Its Latin root *genus*, meaning tribe, is related to the Anglo-Saxon *kin* and *cyng*, both of which contributed to the later word *king*. In other words, to be generous suggests the ability to inspire a sense of nobility in others, recognizing the potential in others.

A Spirit of Renewal

All of our profilees practice renewal in a number of ways. For some, it means changing jobs regularly. For others, it means taking regular sabbaticals from their work during which they rest, renew, and regenerate their minds and hearts. This renewal is particularly important, not just because practitioners of transformational public service work hard. It is important because of the spaces that open up in the renewal process. The tradition of sabbath or sabbatical is rooted in an "earthy sense of sacred work as well as sacred rest" (Waskow, 2004, p. 85). Sacred, restorative rest is essential to transformational public service, whether it be practiced in a way similar to the ancient Hebrew traditions or in other ways.

Doing one's own work or working on oneself is a lifelong, continuous process that brings us, with clarity and wisdom, to the place, in T.S. Eliot's words, where we started, knowing that place for the first time.

Epilogue

Transformational Public Service in the Public Interest

We shall not cease from exploration
And the end of all our exploring
Will be to arrive where we started
And know the place for the first time.

—T.S. Eliot
Four Quartets: Fourth Quartet, "Little Gidding"

We begin this epilogue where we began the book, asking the question, "Can transformational public service help us during a time of significant turmoil and strife?" To repeat our questions, what does it mean to practice transformational public service at this particular moment? Why should we be interested in pursuing transformational public service now?

As we have argued throughout this book, we believe this is an especially important time to reconsider the role of public servants. Indeed, as the scenes from *Waking Life* tell us, "our planet is facing the greatest problems it has ever faced. Ever. We need to be wide awake and dreaming."

Doing so means working to reconnect the public sphere (the collective) to the self (in political terms, the individual) in a deep and significant way. Here, we note particularly the work of Thomas Singer, Bill Bradley, Andrew Samuels, and others who have considered the public sphere from the perspective of depth psychology. In the book *The Vision Thing: Myth, Politics, and Psyche in the World* (Singer, 2000), cutting-edge scholars and practitioners explore politics, leadership, and vision from a mythic level. They are committed to a transformation of politics that can be called the "re-sacralization" of politics—that is, making politics holy, which involves attempting to get a "sense of purpose, decency, aspiration and meaning back into political culture" (Samuels, 2001a, p. 18).

Bradley (2000), for example, asks what happens when the "negative organizing" force of a society disappears. Using the collapse of the Cold War as his focal point, he explores how the dualism of a divided globe pervaded political thinking at all levels—no ambivalence was permitted. It is an unfortunate reality that we, as a nation, seem to need to perpetuate such dualistic thinking—projecting our own shadow characteristics onto the designated "evil empire" of the day, whether that enemy is internal or external opposition.

Singer (2000) suggests that the modern political psyche is in the midst of its own rite of passage. We voice impatience and irritation at facing (presumably) the same issues over and over again. Why do poverty and homelessness continue to coexist with tremendous affluence? Why are attitudes of discrimination, intolerance, and hate so persistent? Yet Singer observes that this iterative pattern—returning to issues over and over again— is a crucial part of the integration process, whether on the individual or national level. Recognizing and addressing complexities of issues is also crucial; oversimplification that leads to single-issue fundamentalism signals psychological and emotional immaturity regardless of one's location on the political spectrum.

Echoing the themes of this book, Singer (2000, p. 3) suggests that we "cultivate the art of not knowing." He notes that this is the same art urged by Keats—what Keats called "negative capability," or the point of deepest (greatest) receptivity and openness. Such receptivity requires us to hold spaces of ambiguity, ambivalence and contradiction for as long as possible—"long enough for something authentic to emerge" (ibid.).

Samuels, too, deplores the psychological condition of the West. In a recent talk, he imagined "the West" as a client (politics "on the couch"):

> Let's take the idea of the West needing therapy a little bit further. What are the particular cultural habits of mind that represent the symptoms of this client, the West? In general terms, I'm thinking about one-sidedness. The way we lack balance, wholeness, and integration, and there is a crisis around those things. But crisis is often the catalyst for healing. I think the ingredients for some kind of healing are there. . . . There is a crisis in our thinking; I'm referring to our binary ways of thinking in pairs of complementary opposites. It goes something like this: if we are rational people, they are irrational; if we are compassionate, they are cruel, and so on. It's this kind of binary thinking which is very difficult to get beyond but I don't pretend to have solved it personally. That makes it very hard to spread a general critique over all the warring players in any conflict-ridden situation, for example the Middle East, and equally makes it very hard to spread a general compassion over them as well. (Samuels, 2004)

As Samuels (2001a) indicates, it has only been in the last few years that psychologists, particularly analytical or depth psychologists, have begun to investigate the relationship between the individual and the political. The founders of analytical and humanistic psychology (Freud, Jung, and Maslow) had ambitions to be of use in the political world, but psychological reductionism got in the way. In his work, Samuels addresses the possibility of forming a new kind of relationship between citizens and the state, one that will release the political energies of people who have withdrawn into their private world out of disgust with the political system as it stands. Samuels calls on psychotherapists to contribute to a transformation of politics by no longer ignoring the demoralization in the political realm and to stop focusing on only personal transformation in their work. He asks therapists to change self-concern into social and political concern, thereby helping to revitalize politics in a way that balances the search for a politics of the internal world with a search for the psychology of the external world. He asks citizens to become the therapists of society—to take what they are learning "on the couch" and apply it to politics.

As citizens, according to Samuels (2001a), we need to balance the politics of the internal world with the politics of the external world. Psychotherapy may help us remodel politics by generating a sense of meaning, not only in private but also in public life. In order to achieve this balance, we need to revise our notions of citizenship, to recognize that being a citizen today requires a conscious familiarity with both the internal and external dimensions of experience. Samuels assumes there is a "politician" within all of us who struggles to develop a degree of political self-awareness that allows the individual to move from personal matters to a sense of social responsibility, developing the capacity to engage as the system permits (if the system permits). This political self-awareness means understanding how our political attitudes have been affected psychologically by our history, experience, family, gender, sexuality, ethnicity, race, nationality, and socioeconomic status and, at the same time, how our personalities have been affected by the political times in which we live.

Moving from individualistic ways of living will require huge value shifts. For instance, Samuels points out, many people believe in sustainable economic development, however we know we cannot have sustainable development without great numbers of people being willing to give up features of their comfortable life—to, at the very least, make some trade-offs. What, says Samuels, other than psychology, will drive such a value shift? "However fascinating it may be to play the parlor game of speculating on the psychological motivations of today's politicians, it may be more significant to find out what would happen to the political system if citizens were to work on their own political self awareness—if they got in touch with the 'politician within' each citizen" (Samuels, 2001b).

Samuels believes that transformative politics requires that we no longer divorce the outer world issues from the personal and subjective lives of the people involved. It is an attempt to generate a new sense of purpose and meaning for both private and public lives. As Samuels says, "Relieved of our feelings of impotence—our inability to change anything—we become less likely to cede our autonomy and agency to others and more likely to take action ourselves" (ibid.).

Part of our political-psychological maturity is being able to integrate light and darkness—or, as Jane Bennett (2001) might put it, to integrate evil and enchantment. As Bennett describes it, enchantment is a sense of openness to the unusual, the captivating, and the disturbing in everyday life. She guides us through a wide and often surprising range of sources of enchantment, showing that we can still find enchantment in nature, for example, but also in such unexpected places as modern technology, advertising, and even bureaucracy. She then explains how everyday moments of enchantment can be cultivated to build an ethics of generosity, stimulating the emotional energy and honing the perceptual refinement necessary to follow moral codes.

Enchantment is a way of viewing the virtual within the actual. It helps us envision a way of behavior within a postmodern world that lacks, at least in this moment, a sense of telos or purpose. Drawing specifically on the tradition of critical theory, Bennett suggests that in a time like ours, when the best we can manage is simply a *weak ontology,* enchantment gives us a framework for forming attachments. Most importantly, these onto-stories, as Bennett (2001, p. 162) calls them, provide a means for bridging (shifting) from deconstruction and nihilism toward a more "articulated, cultivated and affirmed" vision.

Enchantment is not the same as idealism. It is an openness to the unusual, the captivating, and the disturbing in everyday life. With this openness, enchantment helps cultivate a stance of presumptive generosity, motivating acts of understanding.

If, according to Max Weber, the modern age is disenchanted, then, perhaps, the postmodern age calls for re-enchantment. If, when we adopted objective, scientistic thought (as a reaction to dark, pre-enlightenment times) we lost enchantment because the modern "trumped" the religious and/or the aesthetic, perhaps it is time to reconnect with those things we left behind, with wisdom and clarity instead of with blind adherence to dogma or belief systems. If, as everything we cite in this book claims, there is a calling out for transformation in how and why we practice public service (or how/why we live), by what means will this transformation take place?

Nancy Murray (1997, p. 177) tells us that, as public administrators, we need to be "reverently careful in conducting the public's business." Wicked problems and complex situations ask us to be careful (full of care) in our responses and actions. Relying upon Jungian and eastern perspectives, she asks us to be more inclined toward introspection and hesitation and less inclined toward impulsive action, in our "feeble attempt to make things right" (ibid.). Andrew Samuels asks all of us—clients, citizens, and those who "serve" (therapists, social workers, public servants)—to balance the politics of the inner world with the politics of the external world and to consider the congruity (or incongruity) of our values and behaviors (If we believe in sustainability, should we be driving an SUV?).

In 1997, Keshavan Nair wrote a book on leadership, taking his orders from the life of Gandhi. The central premise of Nair's work is that we should all practice, as Gandhi did, one standard of leadership; the same in our private as in our public life. This is no small feat Nair (and Gandhi) is asking of us; some say that even Gandhi struggled to do so. Still, it seems deeply connected to our profilees experiences and the ability to practice everyday enchantment.

What are our projects as practitioners of transformational public service? Be of use; balance your inner and outer worlds; practice passionate detachment; act according to one standard; practice everyday enchantment. Learn to hold contradictions. Be an open, lifelong learner, not afraid to face your shadow and the shadow of others. Learn from your shadow and from the shadows of others. Be a tempered radical. Emulate, if you are not already doing so, those profiled in this book. Dream with your eyes wide open because now, no matter how problematic, is the absolutely most exciting time to be alive and things are just starting.

Dear Readers

We were asked by the readers of our draft manuscript to come back to the book in the end, to bring back our personal voices. Our readers asked us to tell our stories about our own work: to provide an image for how others can do their work.

Admittedly, we have some discomfort with this. Most of the discomfort comes from our belief that there is no one right way to do one's work. The paths are many, as we tried to show earlier. We are all authors of our own stories and they all have their own cadence, tone, setting, and plot. Be the author of your own story. Make it a story you would want to read.

Still, readers will not be surprised to learn that we both have been on a path of individuation for the past few years (through the writing of this book!).

Our paths are different (there are many options), but we are both moving toward a similar place—a place of knowing ourselves well enough so that we can be effective in the world.

These paths began with Jungian analysis and have led to forms of body-work. Headwork is simply not enough and is too deeply embedded in Cartesian notions that artificially separate body, mind, and spirit. One of the most remarkable things about bodywork is that the Cartesian split is turned on its head. Thinking (learning) begins in the body, not in the mind: It is not that I think, therefore I am—it is that I am a body, therefore I think. A friend, who is a practicing attorney, tells the story of his transformation through yoga. His friend said to him, "I love what it does to your body but hate what it has done to your mind." That is the point; the mind follows the body. This is not to say we will achieve states of nirvana or grace (or enlightenment); we still have to live in this world, in these bodies. It is a practice, something one is always working at and toward. Another friend tells a story of the Dalai Lama that ends with this line: "He's not living in Tibet." In other words, sometimes we cannot do that which is most difficult, even if we are called upon by vocation or some higher power to do so. For example, one of the basic premises of Buddhist philosophy and practice is that suffering comes from not recognizing that we (and others) are human—like Dr. Larch from *Cider House Rules* (1994), flawed and lovely creatures. Part of a Buddhist practice is to recognize our humanity and to accept it, all the while we practice the basic guiding principles (and the principles are remarkably similar, regardless of what ancient wisdom practice one embraces: kindness, truthfulness, nonviolence/compassion, non-stealing, responsible behavior, non-harm, and nonattachment).

To practice our work in the public interest, we have to first (and always) practice our work on ourselves.

We have both been quite taken recently with the story of the Sumerian goddess Inanna (Ishtar in the Semitic). In this myth, Inanna must journey into the underworld. At each of the seven gates, she must remove a piece of her stunning regalia (armor). Her regalia—a crown on her head, beads of lapis lazuli around her neck, sparkling stones fastened to her breast, a gold ring around her waist, and a royal robe on her body—represent all of the things with which she used to "arm" herself in the rational world: her intelligence, ambition, creativity, positive feelings, the power to act, a critical ability to judge. "The armor is whatever psychic defenses and walls a person casts up to protect themselves from others" (www.jelder.com/mythology/inanna.html). As she descends into the depths, the armor of consciousness becomes an impediment and she sheds each piece of regalia in turn. Eventually, she becomes like all those who enter the underworld, naked and bowed low. She is dismembered by the Goddess of the Underworld and her corpse is hung on a peg to rot. Eventually, Inanna is able to re-coalesce and return to the upper world, wiser, transformed, and more resilient.

Inanna's journey is the journey of individuation. At each turn in our journey, we, by necessity, shed those things that defined and confined our being in the world. After seeing ourselves as we are, as Inanna saw herself as a corpse, we can rebuild and return. This process is not unlike the process revealed through critical theory—that of deconstructing the received "truths" about our social, political, and economic worlds. Our work requires us to do both—to take apart the reifications of our social, economic, and political worlds *and* to take apart those things we believe to be "true" about ourselves. We hope that this book supports you in your work.

Glossary

archetype/
archetypically

A model or type after which other similar things are patterned. In Jungian psychology, an inherited pattern of thought or symbolic imagery derived from the past collective experience and present in the individual unconscious.

antifoundationalists

Philosophers/scholars who critique the taken-for-granted stance of rational/western philosophy that there is a knowable foundation to the world and events. Antifoundationalists come from a variety of contemporary schools of philosophy including pragmatism, postmodernism, and critical theory.

Cartesian

Relating to René Descartes (French philosopher and scientist, 1596–1650). Best known for his phrase, *Cogito, ergo sum* (I think, therefore I am), Descartes is seen as the father of mechanistic, rationalistic philosophy and science (along with Francis Bacon), which reflects the notion of the superiority of humankind as thinking, rational beings and emphasizes rationalization and logic (a priori) instead of experience (a posteriori).

deductive

Reasoning where something is inferred from a general principle: general to specific, e.g., using principles or theory to explain a particular (rational). Compare to inductive reasoning, where a general principle is inferred from specifics (experience): specific to general, e.g., using a particular (or particulars) to develop principles or theory. Deductive starts somewhere else; inductive starts where you are.

democratic philosophers   From Gramsci, the notion that everyone is a philosopher, thus progressive politics involves change in both thinking and doing. He argued that we all engage in practical activity and within that activity is a conception of the world, or a philosophy. His criterion of progressive politics (transformative politics) stresses the development of popular culture and political organization in such a way that the reification of capitalism can be overcome, in a popular, mass-phenomenon capable of modifying "popular thought [hegemony] and mummified popular culture" (Gramsci, 1971, p. 417).

dialectic   Any systematic reasoning, exposition, or argument that juxtaposes opposed or contradictory ideas and usually seeks to resolve their conflict. A dialectical tension or opposition between two interacting forces or elements.

epistemology/ epistemological   The nature of knowing, the science or grounds of knowledge. How knowing and knowledge are pursued. The branch of philosophy directed toward theories of the origin, sources, and grounds of knowledge. Various foundationalist schools include rationalism and empiricism. Antifoundationalist schools include pragmatism, postmodernism, and some elements of critical theory.

Frankfurt school   The "school" (group of theorists/philosophers), located at the University of Frankfurt, in which contemporary critical theory has its roots.

hegemony   Coercive influence, power, or dominance over others. Interactive: both the powerful and the powerless have to accept and play their prescribed roles. The term was originally applied to the Greek city-states, to describe the dominance of one state over another. It is used in contemporary parlance to include coercively dominant ideas and perspectives that keep institutions and practices in play.

Highlander Research and Education Center	An adult education center, founded by Myles Horton in 1932, for community workers involved in social and economic justice movements. Provides education and support to poor and working people fighting economic injustice, poverty, prejudice, and environmental destruction based upon the founding principle that the answers to the problems facing society lie in the experiences of ordinary people (used by permission from their website, www.highlandercenter.org).
inductive	*See* deductive.
liminal	Of or related to a sensory threshold. Psychologists call liminal space a place where boundaries dissolve and the possibilities of moving across the limits appears—a space of transformation. A period of ambiguity; a marginal or transitional state.
metaphysics	A branch of philosophy concerned with the ultimate nature of existence. The principle area of metaphysical speculation (generally called ontology) is the study of the ultimate (both knowable and unknowable) nature of being. Each philosophic school has its associated metaphysical system.
micrologies	The feminist practice of drawing cultural and political insight from the interplay between the analytic and the subjective-personal. Self-reflexivity in this manner is part of the feminist critique of objectivity and distance.
modernism	The subject from which postmodern philosophy takes its definition. Modernism is associated with rational philosophic schools which assume that all things are knowable through rational or empirical methods, that humans are superior to all other beings and processes because of our rational minds, and that progress is always a viable end.
ontology	A branch of metaphysics (philosophy) concerning the nature and relations of being or existence (e.g., are things fixed or fluid? Subjective or objective?).

organic intellectual   From Antonio Gramsci, who turned the notion of an intellectual away from the "traditional" definition of one who is locked away in an ivory tower, gaining all knowledge and information from books and thinking toward the notion that an intellectual can be born out of experiences, in the fields and on the streets.

political economy   A way of thinking/viewing the world that does not separate politics and economics and rejects a context-free view of economics. With its roots in the theories of Marx (who did not separate politics and economics), it is often a code word for "radical," "alternative," or "leftist."

positivism   A philosophical system that denies any validity to speculation or metaphysics. Maintains that the goal of knowledge is not to explain, but to simply describe the phenomena experienced. Much of contemporary approaches toward knowing (measuring, describing) are based upon positivism or the nineteenth-century extension of logical positivism.

postmodernism   A contemporary philosophical movement (first associated with mid-twentieth-century French philosophers such as Derrida and Foucault) that critiques all that is assumed in modernism, rationalism, and postivism/post-postivism.

praxis   Theoretically informed practical action.

quiescence   Being at rest, inactive. Causing no trouble or symptoms.

radical hillbilly   A term coined by Myles Horton (Highlander school), perhaps with the aid of journalist Bill Moyers, to describe the Appalachian folks Horton worked with at the Highlander school to work toward self-determined radical change for people living in the hills.

reify/reification   To falsely materialize. To make real that which is not.

synchronic   Concerned with the complex events existing in a limited time and ignoring historical antecedents.

Bibliography

Adams, Guy, and Danny Balfour (2004). *Unmasking Administrative Evil.* Revised ed. Armonk, NY: M.E. Sharpe.

Adams, Guy B., and Jay D. White (1994). *Research in Public Administration: Reflections on Theory and Practice.* Thousand Oaks, CA: Sage.

Adorno, Theodor (1966/1973). *Negative Dialectics.* Trans. E.B. Ashton. New York: Seabury Press.

Agger, Benjamin (1991). *A Critical Theory of Public Life: Knowledge, Discourse, and Politics in an Age of Decline.* New York: Falmer Press.

——— (1992). *The Discourse of Domination.* Evanston, IL: Northwestern University Press.

Alford, C. Fred (2001). *Whistleblowers: Broken Lives and Organizational Power.* Ithaca, NY: Cornell University Press.

Alinsky, Saul (1989). *Rules for Radicals.* New York: Vintage.

Arato, Andrew, and Eike Gebhardt (eds.) (1982/1994). *The Essential Frankfurt School Reader.* New York: Continuum.

Argyris, Chris, and Donald A. Schön (1978). *Organizational Learning.* Reading, MA: Addison-Wesley.

Barber, Benjamin R. (1984). *Strong Democracy: Participatory Politics for a New Age.* Berkeley: University of California Press.

Bell, Daniel (1974). *The Coming of Post-Industrial Society.* London: Heinemann.

Bellah, Robert N., Richard Madsen, William M. Sullivan, Ann Swinder, and Steven M. Tipton (1985). *Habits of the Heart: Individualism and Commitment in American Life.* New York: Harper Row.

Bennett, Jane (2001). *The Enchantment of Modern Life: Attachments, Crossings and Ethics.* New Haven, CT: Princeton University Press.

Bennis, Warren G., and Robert J. Thomas (2002a). *Geeks and Geezers.* Cambridge, MA: Harvard University Press.

——— (2002b). "Crucibles of Leadership." *Harvard Business Review* (Sept.) 80(9): 39–45.

Boggs, Carl (1976). *Gramsci's Marxism.* London: Pluto Press.

Bohman, James (1996). "Public Reason and Cultural Pluralism: Political Liberalism and the Problem of Moral Conflict." *Political Theory,* 23(2): 253–79.

Box, Richard C. (2003). "Contradiction, Utopia, and Public Administration." *Administrative Theory & Praxis,* 25(2): 243–60.

——— (2004). *Public Administration and Society: Critical Issues in American Governance.* Armonk, NY: M.E. Sharpe.

Bradley, Bill (2000). "Reflections on Myth, Politics, and Leadership." In T. Singer (ed.), *The Vision Thing: Myth, Politics, and Psyche in the World.* London: Routledge, pp. 23–28.

153

Brooks, David (2001). *Bobos in Paradise: The New Upper Class and How They Got There.* New York: Simon and Schuster.

Carr, Adrian, and Lisa Zanetti (1999). "Metatheorising the Dialectic of Self and Other: The Psychodynamics in Work Organizations." *American Behavioral Scientist,* 43(2): 324–42.

——— (2000). "The Emergence of Surrealism and Its Vital 'Estrangement Effect' in Organization Studies." *Human Relations,* 53(7): 891–921.

Carroll, William, and R.S. Ratner (1994). "Between Leninism and Radical Pluralism: Gramscian Reflections on Counter-hegemony and the New Social Movements." *Critical Sociology,* 20(2): 3–26.

Cohen, David (2001). *Chasing the Red, White, and Blue: A Journey in Tocqueville's Footsteps Through Contemporary America.* New York: Picador USA.

Couto, Richard A. (1993). "Narrative, Free Space, and Political Leadership in Social Movements." *Journal of Politics,* 53(1): 57–79.

Dahl, Robert A. (1956). *A Preface to Democratic Theory.* Chicago: University of Chicago Press.

Das, Lama Surya (2003). *Letting Go of the Person You Used to Be.* New York: Broadway Books.

Denhardt, Robert B. (1981). *In the Shadow of Organization.* Lawrence, KS: Regents Press of Kansas.

Denhardt, Robert B., and Maria P. Aristigueta (1996). "Developing Intrapersonal Skills." In J.L. Perry (ed.), *Handbook of Public Administration.* San Francisco: Jossey-Bass, pp. 682–96.

Denhardt, Robert B., Janet Vinzant Denhardt, and Maria P. Aristigueta (2002). *Managing Human Behavior in Public and Nonprofit Organizations.* Thousand Oaks, CA: Sage.

Denhardt, Janet V., and Robert B. Denhardt (2003). *The New Public Service: Serving, Not Steering.* Armonk, NY: M.E. Sharpe.

Dickstein, Morris (ed.) (1998). *The Revival of Pragmatism: New Essays on Social Thought, Law, and Culture.* Durham, NC: Duke University Press.

Disch, Lisa J. (1993). "More Truth Than Fact: Storytelling as Critical Understanding in the Writings of Hannah Arendt." *Political Theory,* 21(4): 665–94.

Farmer, David John (2003). "Power of Refusal: Introduction to the Symposium." *Administrative Theory & Praxis,* 25(2): 173–82.

Fischer, Frank (2000). *Citizens, Experts, and the Environment: The Politics of Local Knowledge.* Durham, NC: Duke University Press.

——— (2003). *Reframing Public Policy: Discursive Politics and Deliberative Practices.* New York: Oxford University Press.

Fontana, Benedetto (1993). *Hegemony and Power: On the Relation Between Gramsci and Machiavelli.* Minneapolis: University of Minnesota Press.

Foucault, Michel (1980). *Power/Knowledge.* New York: Pantheon.

——— (1984). *The Foucault Reader.* New York: Pantheon.

Fox, Charles J. (2003). "The Prosecutorial State." *Administrative Theory & Praxis,* 25(4): 63–90.

Freire, Paulo (1970/2000). *Pedagogy of the Oppressed.* 30th anniversary edition. New York: Continuum.

Freud, Sigmund (1913/1975). *Totem and Taboo. Standard Edition of the Complete Psychological Works of Sigmund Freud,* vol. 13. Trans. James Strachey. London: Hogarth Press.

———— (1930/1975). *Civilization and Its Discontents. Standard Edition of the Complete Psychological Works of Sigmund Freud,* vol. 21. Trans. James Strachey. London: Hogarth Press.

Fromm, Erich (1976). *To Have or To Be.* New York: Harper Row.

———— (1979). *To Have or To Be?* London: Abacus.

Galbraith, John Kenneth (1967). *The New Industrial State.* Boston: Houghton Mifflin.

Galston, William (2002). *Liberal Pluralism: The Implications of Value Pluralism for Political Theory and Practice.* Cambridge, UK: Cambridge University Press.

Gaventa, John (1980). *Power and Powerlessness.* Chicago: University of Illinois Press.

———— (1993). "The Powerful, the Powerless, and the Experts: Knowledge Struggles in an Information Age." In P. Park, M. Brydon-Miller, B. Hall, and T. Jackson (eds.), *Voices of Change: Participatory Research.* Toronto: OISE Press, pp. 21–40.

Giroux, Henry (1983). *Theory and Resistance in Education: A Pedagogy for the Opposition.* South Hadley, MA: Bergin and Garvey.

———— (1988). *Schooling and the Struggle for Public Life: Critical Pedagogy in the Modern Age.* Minneapolis: University of Minnesota Press.

Gladwell, Malcom (2002). *The Tipping Point: How Little Things Can Make a Big Difference.* New York: Back Bay Books.

Glassner, Barry (2000). *The Culture of Fear: Why Americans Are Afraid of the Wrong Things.* New York: HarperCollins.

Gramsci, Antonio (1971). *Selections from the Prison Notebooks.* Trans. and ed. Q. Hoare and G. Nowell-Smith. London: Lawrence and Wishart.

Guba, Egon, and Yvonna S. Lincoln (1994). "Competing Paradigms in Qualitative Research." In N. Denzin and Y. Lincoln (eds.), *Handbook of Qualitative Research.* Thousand Oaks, CA: Sage, pp. 105–17.

Haraway, Donna (1991). *Simians, Cyborgs, and Women: The Reinvention of Nature.* New York: Routledge, pp. 183–201.

Hauke, Christopher (2001). *Jung and the Postmodern: The Interpretation of Realities.* London: Routledge.

Heying, Charles (1999). "Autonomy vs. Solidarity: Liberal, Totalitarian, and Communitarian Traditions." *Administrative Theory & Praxis,* 21(1): 39–50.

Hollis, James (1993). *The Middle Passage: From Misery to Meaning in Midlife.* Toronto: Inner City Books.

———— (1994). *Under Saturn's Shadow: The Wounding and Healing of Men.* Toronto: Inner City Books.

———— (2001). *Creating a Life: Finding Your Individual Path.* Toronto: Inner City Books.

Holub, Renate (1992). *Antonio Gramsci: Beyond Marxism and Postmodernism.* New York: Routledge.

Horkheimer, Max (1937/1976). *Critical Theory: Selected Essays.* New York: Seabury Press.

Horkheimer, Max, and Theodor Adorno (1944/1972). *Dialectic of Enlightenment.* New York: Seabury Press.

Irving, John (1994). *Cider House Rules.* New York: Ballantine.

Jameson, Frederic (1971). *Marxism and Form.* Princeton, NJ: Princeton University Press.

Johnson, Robert, and Jerry M. Ruhl (1998). *Balancing Heaven and Earth: A Memoir of Visions, Dreams and Realizations.* San Francisco: HarperCollins.

Kemmis, Daniel (1990). *Community and the Politics of Place.* Norman: University of Oklahoma Press.

Kempton, Sally (2004). "Just Let Go." *Yoga Journal* (May/June): 75–80.

Kimball, Rogers (2000). "Tocqueville Today." *New Criterion,* 19(3), www.newcriterion.com/archive/19/nov00/tocque.htm. Date accessed: September 2003.

Kincheloe, Joe L., and Peter L. McLaren (1994). "Rethinking Critical Theory and Qualitative Research." In Norman Denzin and Yvonna S. Lincoln (eds.), *Handbook of Qualitative Research.* Thousand Oaks, CA: Sage, pp. 138–57.

King, Cheryl Simrell (1998). "Reflective Scholarship: Healing the Scholarship/Practice Wounds." *Administrative Theory & Praxis,* 20(2): 159–71.

King, Cheryl Simrell, and Camilla Stivers, in collaboration with Richard C. Box et al. (1998). *Government Is Us: Public Administration in an Anti-Government Era.* Thousand Oaks, CA: Sage.

Kouzes, James M., and Barry Z. Pozner (1995). *The Leadership Challenge.* San Francisco: Jossey-Bass.

Kristeva, Julia (1982). *Strangers to Ourselves.* New York: Columbia University Press.

Krugman, Paul (2002). "The End of Middle-Class America (and the Triumph of the Plutocrats)." *New York Times Magazine* (Oct. 20).

Light, Paul (1999). *The New Public Service.* Washington, DC: Brookings Institution.

Lipset, Seymour Martin, and Gary Marks (2000). *It Didn't Happen Here: Why Socialism Failed in the United States.* New York: Norton.

Lowi, Theodore (1979). *The End of Liberalism: The Second Republic of the United States.* New York: Norton.

Lubrano, Alfred (2003). *Limbo.* New York: Wiley and Sons.

Lukes, Steven (1974). *Power: A Radical View.* London: Macmillan.

Manchester, William (1993). *A World Lit Only by Fire: The Mediaeval Mind and the Renaissance–Portrait of an Age.* Boston: Back Bay Books.

McSwite, O.C. (2002). *Invitation to Public Administration.* Armonk, NY: M.E. Sharpe.

Marcuse, Herbert (1941/1960). *Reason and Revolution.* Boston: Beacon Press.

———— (1955/1960). *Eros and Civilization: A Philosophical Inquiry into Freud.* Boston: Beacon Press.

———— (1964). *One Dimensional Man: Studies in the Ideology of Advanced Industrial Society.* London: Routledge and Kegan Paul.

———— (1970). *Five Lectures: Psychoanalysis, Politics and Utopia.* Boston: Beacon Press.

———— (unknown/1993). "Some Remarks on Aragon: Art and Politics in the Totalitarian Era." *Theory, Culture & Society,* 10(2): 181–95.

Mayo, Peter (1999). *Gramsci, Freire, and Adult Education: Possibilities for Transformative Action.* London: Zed Books.

Merrifield, Juliet (1993). "Putting Scientists in Their Place: Participatory Research in Environmental and Occupational Health." In P. Park, M. Brydon-Miller, B. Hall, and T. Jackson (eds.), *Voices of Change: Participatory Research.* Toronto: OISE Press, pp. 65–84.

McLuhan, Marshall (1960). Broadcast interview with CBC News. Retrieved from http://archives.cbc.ca/400d.asp?id=1–69–342–1814andwm6=1. Date accessed March 2004.

McSwite, O.C. (2002). *Invitation to Public Administration.* Armonk, NY: M.E. Sharpe.

Meyerson, Debra E. (2001). *Tempered Radicals: How People Use Difference to Inspire Change at Work.* Cambridge, MA: Harvard Business School Press.

Moore, Mark (2000). *Creating Public Value: Strategic Management in Government.* Cambridge, MA: Harvard University Press.

Morris, David (1999). "Small is Still Beautiful." *Utne Reader,* 93 (May/June): 24–27.

Moyer, Bill, Joann McAllister, Mary Lou Finley, and Steve Soifer (2002). *Doing Democracy: The MAP Model for Organizing Social Movements.* Gabriola Island, BC: New Society Press.

Murray, Nancy (1997). *An Inner Voice for Public Administration.* Westport, CT: Praeger.

Myss, Caroline (2001). *Sacred Contracts: Awakening Your Divine Potential.* New York: Three Rivers Press.

Nair, Keshavan (1997). *A Higher Standard of Leadership: Lessons from the Life of Gandhi.* San Francisco: Berrett-Koehler.

Palmer, Parker (2000). *Let Your Life Speak: Listening for the Voice of Vocation.* San Francisco: Jossey-Bass.

Patterson, Patricia (2001). "Imagining Anti-Administration's Anti-Hero." *Administrative Theory & Praxis,* 23(4): 529–40.

Peirce, Charles Saunders (1877/1977). "The Fixation of Belief." In Louis Menand (ed.) *Pragmatism: A Reader.* New York: Vintage Books, pp. 7–25.

Perera, Sylvia Brinton (1981). *Descent of the Goddess: A Way of Initiation for Women.* Toronto: Inner City Books.

——— (1986). *The Scapegoat Complex: Toward a Mythology of Shadow and Guilt.* Toronto: Inner City Books.

Phillips, Kevin (2003). *Wealth and Democracy: A Political History of the American Rich.* New York: Broadway Books.

Popper, Karl (1963). *Conjectures and Refutations.* New York: HarperTorch.

Prilleltensky, Isacc and Dennis Fox (1997). "Introducing Critical Psychology: Values, Assumptions, and the Status Quo." In Dennis Fox and Isacc Prilleltensky, *Critical Psychology: An Introduction.* London: Sage, pp. 117–30.

Reich, Robert B. (1991). *Public Management in a Democratic Society.* Englewood Cliffs, NJ: Prentice Hall.

Ricci, David (1984). *The Tragedy of Political Science.* New Haven, CT: Yale University Press.

Rosen, Jeffery (1997). "Introduction: Jung and the Post-Jungians." In Polly Young-Eisendrath and Terence Dawson (eds.), *Cambridge Companion to Jung.* Cambridge, UK: Cambridge University Press, pp. 1–15.

——— (2001a). *Politics on the Couch: Citizenship and the Internal Life.* London: Profile Books.

——— (2001b). "Politics on the Couch." www.cgjungpage.org/content/view/72/78.

——— (2004). "Can Citizens Be Therapists of the World?" *Lapis Magazine.Org.* www.lapismagazine.org/samuels.html. Date accessed March 2004.

——— (2004). "Naked Terror." *New York Times Magazine* (Jan. 4).

Schattschneider, Elmer Eric (1960). *The Semisovereign People: A Realist's View of Democracy in America.* New York: Holt, Rinehart, and Winston.

Sell, Christina (2003). *Yoga from the Inside Out: Making Peace with Your Body Through Yoga.* Berkeley, CA: Rodmell Press.

Singer, Thomas (ed.) (2000). *The Vision Thing: Myth, Politics, and Psyche in the World.* London: Routledge.

Spicer, Michael (2004). "Masks of Freedom: An Examination of Isaiah Berlin's Ideas on Freedom and Their Implications for Public Administration." *Administrative Theory & Praxis,* 25(4): 545–88.

Stone, Deborah (2001). *Policy Paradox: The Art of Political Decision Making.* Revised ed. New York: W.W. Norton.

Thornham, Sue (1997). *Passionate Detachments: An Introduction to Feminist Film Theory.* London: Oxford University Press.

Tocqueville, Alexis de (1839/2001). *Democracy in America.* New York: Signet.

Turner, Bryan S. (1986). *Citizenship and Capitalism: The Debate over Reformism.* London: Allen and Unwin.

Twine, Fred (1994). *Citizenship and Social Rights: The Interdependence of Self and Society.* London: Sage.

Walker, Margaret Urban (1997). *Moral Understandings: A Feminist Study in Ethics.* London: Routledge.

Waskow, Arthur (2004). "Reclaiming Our Day of Rest: Why We Should Keep the Sabbath." *Utne Reader* (Feb.).

West, Cornell (1991). *The Ethical Dimensions of Marxist Thought.* New York: Monthly Review.

——— (1995). "Theory, Pragmatisms, and Politics." In Robert Hollinger and David Depew (eds.) *Pragmatism: From Progressivism to Postmodernism.* Westport, CT: Praeger, pp. 314–26.

Whitebook, Joel (1995). *Perversion and Utopia: A Study in Psychoanalysis and Critical Theory.* Cambridge, MA: MIT Press.

Witherell, Carol, and Nell Noddings (1991). "Prologue: An Invitation to Our Readers." In C. Witherell and N. Noddings (eds.), *Stories Lives Tell: Narrative and Dialogue in Education.* New York: Teachers College Press, pp. 1–12.

Woodman, Marion (1992). *Leaving My Father's House: A Journey to Conscious Femininity.* Boston: Shambhala.

"You Bought, They Sold." (2002). *Fortune Magazine* (Sept. 2).

Young-Eisendrath, Polly (1995). "Gender and Individuation: Relating to Self and Other." In Dolores Elise Brien (ed.), *Mirrors of Transformation: The Self in Relationships.* Berwyn, PA: The Round Table Press, pp. 13–20.

Zanetti, Lisa A. (1997). "Advancing Praxis: Connecting Critical Theory with Practice in Public Administration." *American Review of Public Administration,* 27(2): 145–67.

——— (1998). "At the Nexus of State and Civil Society: The Transformative Practice of Public Administration." In Cheryl Simrell King, Camilla Stivers, and collaborators, *Government Is Us: Public Administration in an Anti-Government Era.* Thousand Oaks, CA: Sage, pp. 102–21.

——— (2002). "Leaving Our Father's House: Micrologies, Archetypes, and Fear of Conscious Femininity in Organizational Contexts." *Journal of Organizational Change Management* 15(5): 523–37.

Zanetti, Lisa, and Adrian Carr (1998). "Exploring the Psychodynamics of Political Change." *Administrative Theory & Praxis,* 20(3): 358–73.

Zipes, Jack (1995). *Creative Storytelling: Building Community, Changing Lives.* New York: Routledge.

Index

About the Authors

Cheryl Simrell King, Ph.D., is a member of the faculty of The Evergreen State College, teaching primarily in the graduate program in Public Administration (MPA). Coauthor of *Government Is Us: Public Administration in an Anti-Government Era* (1998), as well as articles in trade press and academic journals, she writes and practices in the areas of democratizing and transforming public administration, accountability, and the relationships among and between citizens and their governments.

Lisa A. Zanetti is an associate professor in the Harry S Truman School of Public Affairs at the University of Missouri-Columbia. She is a certified mediator and often uses Theatre of the Oppressed techniques to teach conflict resolution. Her work on critical theory and public administration is known nationally and internationally, and has appeared in a variety of journals including the *American Review of Public Administration, Administration & Society, American Behavioral Scientist, Administrative Theory & Praxis, Journal of Organizational Change Management,* and *Human Relations.* She has a forthcoming chapter in *The Passion of Organizing.* Before entering academe Dr. Zanetti was employed as an international trade specialist at the U.S. Department of Commerce and the U.S. International Trade Commission.